Robert Fleming

The Confirming Worke of Religion

In its Necessity and Use Briefly Held Forth

Robert Fleming

The Confirming Worke of Religion
In its Necessity and Use Briefly Held Forth

ISBN/EAN: 9783337715632

Printed in Europe, USA, Canada, Australia, Japan

Cover: Foto ©Lupo / pixelio.de

More available books at **www.hansebooks.com**

THE
CONFIRMING WORKE
OF
RELIGION,

In its neceſſity and uſe, briefly held forth; that
each Chriſtian may have a proper *ballaſt* of his
own, of the grounds and reaſons of his
faith, and thus ſee the greatneſſe of that
ſecurity, on which he adventures
his eternal ſtate,

OR

The true and infallible way, for attaining a *confirmed ſtate* in Religion, from theſe primary evidences and demonſtrations of our faith; which the
Lord hath himſelf given, ſo as it may be eaſy for
the meaneſt in the Church to know the ſame,
and be ready to render an account
thereof to all that ask.
With a ſhort and confirming proſpect of the
work of the Lord about his Church,
in theſe laſt times.

BY
R. FLEMING,
Miniſter of the Goſpel of Chriſt.

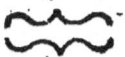

At ROTTERDAM,
Printed by REINIER LEERS,
M. DC. LXXXV.

The PREFACE.

His *small Essay, here offered, is on the greatest subject, can fall under the consideration of mankind; and is a study, was never more pressingly called for, then in these dayes,* for men to be making peace with God, and to have such an assurance of his truth, as can fully quiet and support the soul, though all sensible props should be brocken, and fail. Great changes doe surely hasten on this generation, and the life of faith, is in an other manner like to be put to tryal, then since the Churches rise and recovery from Antichristian bondage. The storme now visibly grows upon the Churches of Christ, though nothing is thus to faint or shake, the spirits of any, who know their anchor is sure and cast within the vail; but the strongest difficulties, in following the Lord, when overcome, yeelds the greatest victory, and will be not only matter of joy here, but to all eternity, in having with patience and hope indured, and got well through a throng of temptations and assaults in a resolute adherence to the truth. If men think it their wisdome to secure their private interest, by dividing it in such a time from the publick cause of the Reformed Church, and make light of the greatest truths of God now assaulted, of the blood of the Martyrs, yea of their own eternal state, by any coolnesse or shrin-

* 2
king

king from the same; they will find no temporal motives, can ever compense that losse and ruine which inevitably will meet such in the issue, yea that these words of Mordecai to Esther, Esth.4; 13, 14. have the same voice, and weight in this day. What is held forth in the following worke, I may with humble confidence say, was under some pressure to have such clear evidence and quieting persuasion of divine truth, as made it lesse easy to have my own spirit satisfyed herein, then possibly it may be to others; for if it were not from that blessed assurance of the Lords being God, of the revelation of Christ, and of the glory to come, I should not know what could be conforting or make a rational being desireable. Some singulare ingadgments I judge my self also to stand under; for putting to my seal to the truth and faithfulnesse of God in his word, from many signal confirmations hereof in the course of my pilgrimage; if such a poor testimony might be of any weight. Let the blessed Lord, gratiously accept this small offering to him, and for the interest of his truth, by so mean an instrument, and give some fruit hereof, that may abide, and be found in the day of Christ.

I hope the Reader may find by a perusal of the I. Chap. of what serious use and intent the II. is; yea that in this day it was not unseasonable or incongruous to the forgoing subject what is held forth in the III. Chapter. But oh it is sad and amazing to think how few are under that weight of Religion, as once to have a serious inquiry on the grounds and reasons thereof, and to accompt the most special assistances to their faith to be the greatest helpers of their joy within time.

The

THE
True and infallible
W A Y
For attaining a confirmed state
in RELIGION, &c.

CHAPTER I.

The Primitive Confirmation in the truth of Christianity, held forth and cleared, in its continued necessity and use to this day, in a few Positions.

posit. I.

That nothing can have a more sad and threatning aspect on the present state of religion in all the churches of Christ, then that utter estrangment, most are under, to the true grounds of faith, and to those foundamental differences betwixt Christianity, & every false way, which no pretended religion can lay claim to. The reasons of the *Position*, are these. I. That it is too visibly manifest, how no men in the

A   world

world know fo little of their own profeffion, were it of any human art or fcience,
as fuch who bear the name of Chriftians, or
are fo generally ftrangers to the truth and
firmneffe of the principles therof, for main-
taining either a due valuation, or powerful
fenfe of the fame on their foul ; fo, that an
implicit and *traditional profeffion* is the only
part and propriety which moft can claim in
the truth , and doctrine they profeffe.
II. That fo rare alfo is any fuch ferious worke
amonghft men , as a perfonal inquiry and
tryal, if there be indeed fuch a thing as an
experimental and foul quickning religion in the
earth, that can bear the expenfe of the moft
difmal and afflicting times, and hath fo great
a temporal revenue lying therto, as peace
with God, an immediate communion with
him, the joy and comforts of the *H. Ghoſt*,
when under fuch preffours of trouble as are
above the fupport of nature. III. That
the furtheft account, why moft goe under
the name of Chriftians, rather then of any
other forme, can rife no higher then cufto-
me and education, that it did befpeak them
from their birth , and was the religion of
their anceftours, yea become in that manner naturall to them , as the cuftomes and
language of their country ; which are
grounds that should determine to the very
oppo-

oppofite profeffion, if they were ftated under the fame circumftances, and had the fame motives to be *Mahumetans*; fince it is
fure thefe can found no other affent, then is
fuitable to the nature and ftrenth therof
I V. That thus it cannot be under debate,
how the moft numerous part of vifible pro-
feffours, are fo deftitute of any defenfe from
internal motives, and folid conviction of
the truth they profeffe, upon its own evidence; as there was never more caufe to fear,
fome unufual apoftacy from the very vifible
profeffion of Chrift, upon any violent tryal and affault this way, when fuch finds it
more eafy to render up their religion, then
to adhere to the fame, under ftrongh temptations, who yet never knew that fubftance,
advantage, or certainty herein, as could
preponderate with the want of all external
motives for fuch a profeffion.

That thus one of the higheft fervices of *Pofit. III*
thefe times, for the publik good of the
Church, does convincingly lye here; to
have *the faith of affent* to the truth and doctrine of Chrift, in a clear and firme certainty of the judgment, on its own evidence,
more vigoroufly promot, and the proper
means and affiftances, which the Lord hath
given for this end, in fome other manner
yet improven, then feems to be this day;

for

for a more univerſal uſe. The grounds to
inforce the neceſſity hereof , are theſe; I.
that its ſure wherever the Goſpel is revealed
to men , it comes with ſo full an aſſurance
of underſtanding , and ſufficiency of objective evidence , as can admit no poſſible
doubtfulneſſe herein , which is the credit
and glory of our religion , that in no other
way it doth require acceptance , but with
the furtheſt conviction of evidence. II. Becauſe the expreſſe deſigne and tendency of
this bleſſed revelation , is no leſſe to found
ſuch a *rational aſſurance* in the judgment, of
its truth , then to ingadge their will and conſent , for imbracing therof ; and though
ſuch great demonſtrations for this end
can only , *in ſuo genere* , have a convincing
influence to perſwade the underſtanding,
yet are they of ſuch weight here , as next to
the demonſtration of the Spirit of God,
they are the greateſt means to bring up mens
aſſent to a full and quieting reſt on that ſecurity to which they muſt concredite themſelves for ever, and to let them ſee , that
this even here by the way , is aſſuredly full,
though not yet their injoyment. III. Becauſe this faith of aſſent , ſhould be firſt followed in the order of nature , as being the
very firſt principle of converſion , to know
and be ſure, that God hath ſent his ſon into
the

the world to fave finners; wherin as the *H.*
Ghoft is not the objective , but the efficient
caufe here of our faith, fo is not the internal worke and teftimony he gives on the foul
the firft teftimony, but muft ftill have refpect to the revelation of the word without,
and fuch demonftrative evidences therof,
wherwith it is revealed to the world, nor
may ever be feparate, that which God hath
himfelf fo indiffolubly joyned. · I V. That
fo convincing a neceffity and ufe is hereof to
the Church, and in a fpecial way with refpect to the youth, for a more firme laying
of the groundwork of their Chriftian profeffion , and to be as the feed-plot of a bleffed and defirable grouth amonghft fuch in
this day; that they might thus know early,
fomething of thefe primary grounds and demonftrations of their faith; fo alfo is it a ftudy of that high importance, as I humbly judge, should be of notable ufe for a Manuduc-
tion in the firft place to ftudents of *Divinity*,
before they launch forth in that vaft and im-
menfe ocean of the fpeculative part therof;
and for being at fome greater advantage
thus for carying on fuch a confirming worke
in the Church in their future fervice. V. Yea
of what ufe might this be with refpect to
many, who may be fore haunted, with hid
and dreadful temptations to infidelity, and

to weaken them on the very foundations of their faith; who are wholly unfurnished of any such grounds and arguments in their judgment to repel the same : and it is sure, to believe firmly the history of the Gospel, *that God was manifested in our nature*, to save man , is with respect to the object a much higher act of faith, then to believe, that he will save us; since as the one doth unspeakably more transcend all human reason then the other , so doth the Apostle thus argue from the greater to the lesse, Rom. 8: 32. *That he who gave his own son to the death ; will he not also with him give us all things.*

Posit. III.   That such a confirming worke, was most specially followed in the practize of the primitive times , and one of the great ends of the ministry of the *Apostles and Evangelists*, to have this faith of assent and doctrinal certainty therof, on its proper grounds and evidences , deeply founded in mens judgment; is so clear, as cannot come under debate. I. That this way did the great author of our profession himself take , not only by the authority of his word , and the power and energy of grace , but with that convincing evidence and demonstration of his truth to mens understanding, as might found also a firme and rational assurance hereof. II. That for this end, he did pray
the

the Father, *Joh.* 17: 21. and was fo much prefled herein, that fo great an external demonftration of the truth of the Gofpel, in the concord and unity of his people, might be kept clear, that the world might thus believe that he was fent of God, and have a deeper conviction hereof ferved on them, by fuch an evidence. III. That one fpecial intent of the Evangel of Luke, was for this end, *Luke* 1: 4. that men might know not only the things themfelves by a naked relatation, but the certainty of thefe things, wherin they had been formerly inftructed. IV. That herein did the miniftry of *Apollos* fo brightly shine forth, *Act.* 18:28. and was then of moft fingulare ufe to the Church, by that clearneffe of rational conviction and demonftrative arguments for the truth of Chrift, as the greateft gainfayers could not withftand. V. That its fure it was then without exception, expreffly required of the meaneft within the Church, to be allways ready to render the reafons of their hope to all who ask; and not only to know what they did believe, but why they did fo, as is clear 1 *Pet.* 3: 15. yea that this could not be by bringing forth of internal evidences, for conviction of others, but to give them an account of the moft cogent grounds and demonftrations of the Gofpel,

as

as might be moſt prevalent, and confirming
to the weak, and leave others inexcuſable;
and ſeems to have been then ſpecially preſſed in theſe primitive times, as a proper teſt
of their Chriſtian profeſſion. V I. And we
ſee herein alſo, how much theſe excellent
Bereans were taken up, and were ſo highly
commended of the *H. Ghoſt*, *Act*. 17: 11.
to know the *demonſtrative* part of Chriſtianity., and by its own evidence, with that
intire harmony and conſent of the Scripture
therin, and their being thus diligently intent in that comparing-worke of religion,
to ſee the truth therof not ſingly and apart
by themſelves alone, but in that joynt union
and coherence, wherin they ſtand, each in
their own room, for confirming and giving
light to other. V I I. That this was the
way alſo, wherin the Goſpel did come to
the Gentil church is cleerly ſhewed 1 *Theſſ.*
1: 5. *Not in word only, but as in power, and
in the H. Ghoſt, ſo alſo in much aſſurance of underſtanding, upon its own evidence*; which
was that way, it did ſo wonderfully
prevail over the world againſt nature, and
ſtream of fleſh and blood, that ſtood in the
furtheſt oppoſition therto. V I I I. That
one of the greateſt ſervices of the Apoſtles in
their viſiting the Churches, did expreſly ly
here *Acts* 14: 22. to confirme the ſouls of
the

the Disciples in the firſt place on the certainty of their faith, and then in exhorting
them to continue in the ſame, ſo as they
might follow the Lord, with the furtheſt light and aſſurance of mind, amidſt
the great tryalls of ſuch a time. IX. That
its this way alſo the world is rendred inexcuſable for their misbeliefe of the Goſpel,
when under ſuch ſufficiency of means given
for this end, by ſo great a diſcovery of the
confirming evidences of its truth, ſo as they
can have no pretence herein, but an obſtinacy and reſolution not to be convinced;
on which ground doth our bleſſed Lord
teſtify, that it was no want of light, upon
the certainty of his truth, why men did not
receive it, but that they loved darkneſſe
better then light, becauſe their deeds were
evil; & when ſuch clear, rational, and convincing evidences are laid open to their view,
how moſt poſſibly can get theſe put by or
rejected, is not eaſy to comprehend, but
that a real irritation and torment of ſpirit,
from ſuch clearneſſe of evidence, doth thus
more tend to harden then convince.

    That there is a continued neceſſity of ſuch *Poſit.*
a confirmation in the faith to this day, what *IV.*
ever can be objected of ſo long a conſent
and preſcription of time in the profeſſion
therof, is fully demonſtrable on theſe
grounds.

grounds. I. Becaufe it is fure, the Chriftian faith doth ftill need thefe affiftances ; and is a ftrang miftake , that only for *Heathens , and Atheifts* , fuch confirming evidences of the fame fhould be adduced, but not for any under a vifible profeffion, when the whole of *divinity* , and *doctrine* of *our faith* , is fo full of demonftrative arguments, for the dayly ufe of the moft eftablished Chriftians in their paffage through time. II. That as the higheft motives to all ferious godlineffe and the moral duties of Chriftianity muft needs be from its known certainty to us, fo is the continued ufe therof to be ftill the fame. III. That thefe numerous tryalls and conflicts of Chriftians now, doe no leffe call for fome higher eftablishment in the truth on which they muft alone reft , when all vifible props fail in their judgmens, then of fupporting grace; nor is it conceavable how men can this day walk in the light of any true joy and comfort, without a more follid affurance of their being on fafe grounds herein then moft feem to reckon. IV. Becaufe the revelation of the Gofpel and of an eternal ftate in an other world, is fo great and wonderfull as its ftrang how this is not the higheft intereft of mens life , to have their faith more deeply confirmed on the furtheft tryal of their fecurity now

by

by the way herein, who muſt ſhortly make
ſo great a tryal therof at death ; for if we were but once this lenth to ask our own ſoul,
what the *Chriſtian faith* indeed is, and are
thus called to believe, it could not poſſibly
but beget ſome extaſy of wondering at the
greatneſſe therof, and to reckon any light
and implicit aſſent to the ſame as a degree
both of Atheiſm & indifferency in this matter.   V. Though there be no conflict with
Heathens as in the *firſt times*, yet was ſuch a
ſpirit never more aloft then it is now to take
of all firm aſſent to the greateſt principles of
truth, when *Atheiſme* ſeems to be at its *ultimus conatus* in the world, and we are fallen
in ſo amazing an hower of the power of darkneſſe as makes theſe latter times more remarkably perillous and trying then the firſt.
V I. Yea if ſuch a confirming worke, be
one of the greateſt means to advance the repute and honour of religion, when its won-
ted awe and veneration is ſo far loſt, and to
awake men to deeper impreſſions of its
truth, when ſo few ſeeme now under any
ſuch weight ; then it is ſure there was never
more need of the ſame then in this day.

   That ſuch a ſervice to the *Church*, doth *Poſit. V.*
not only reſpect the more knowing, inquiſitive, and judicious part therof, but the
meaneſt profeſſours of religion alſo, of
                                whom

whom this is neceſſarly required, is evident on theſe *grounds*. I. Becauſe each Chriſtian should have undoubtedly ſuch a *ballaſt* on their own ſoul, of the ſolid and rational grounds of their faith, as well as theſe of greater parts and induments : the promotting of which were it more deeply conſidered, I dare humbly adventure to ſay, should be found one of the choiceſt meanes to promot Chriſtianity this day. I I. Becauſe this is not to drive any to doubt or queſtion the leaſt ſincere degree of *aſſent*, though it be not with ſuch ſtrenght of evidence as in others, nor can by that formal argumentation give the ſame accompt therof; ſince a few grounds this way may ſpecially help to ſome ſolid conviction and confirming of their mind, when they may be ignorant of many other cogent arguments for this end; but its ſure alſo the greater clearneſſe of evidence doth ſtill in the appointed way of means lead into a more firme and ſtrong aſſent of the judgment, to the truth of our religion. I I I. Becaus the ſtrenth of the foundation in it ſelf cannot be enough if it be not with ſuch a known evidence, as men may build firmly and with aſſurance theron; nor hath the Lord thus only deſigned to give his people an infaillible and ſure teſtimony to adventure on, but that it should be

made

made fure alfo to them. IV. Becaufe none
can in truth fay that *Jefus is the Lord but by
the H. Ghoft*, 1 *Cor.* 22: 3. by which is not
to be underftood fo much there, the neceffity of fupernatural grace, for a faving faith,
but that none can give a true affent and con-
feffion of the fame, but from thefe grounds
and arguments which are revealed by the *H.
Ghoft* unto men for this end; and as its fure
that thefe *charaƈters and evidences of divinity,*
which are imprinted on the whole revelation of the Gofpel, may be clear & demonftrative to our judgment, fo are they as truly *divine*, as the doƈtrine which is confirmed
therby. V. Becaufe there can be no poffible caufe for credulity of the truth from
any intricate obfcureneffe of the fame, when
the Lord hath given fuch great affiftances to
our faith to be *as milk for babes* as wel as *meat
to ftrong men*. And though it be objeƈted
that the furtheft objeƈtive evidence of the
Gofpel, with fo clear and ftrong a conveyance therof, is yet fo little operative on moft;
the fame might be faid alfo of the whole letter of the Scripture; but as this tends not in
the leaft to refolve our religion into any
meer exercife of reafon, and leaves the whole worke of the Spirit, in its energy and ope-
ration therwith on mens fouls, intire; yet
doth it fully evince fuch a fufficiency of evi-
den-

dence with the Chriſtian faith, as makes any
doubtfulneſſe herein ſimply impoſſible,
through want of the greateſt advantage of
means; yea ſuch as are of another kind then
to induce only a *probable perſwaſion* of the ſame. VI. Becauſe it is one of the ſaddeſt ſymp-
tomes of the preſent ſtate of religion, that
ſo few almoſt in whole congregations can
give any clear aſſent to the truth and certainty thereof, but to amazment both live and
dye ſtrangers to the ſame, yea how many
of theſe who are otherwiſe ſerious in religion, yet have their *faith ſtarved* this way,
and are deſtitute of any ſuch ſupport; but
as it is not the *numberouſneſſe of profeſſours,*
but the *ſtrength and ſolidity of their faith,*
wherein the Churches ſtrength moſt lyes,
and hath more flowriſhed in a few ſuch to
beget a greater awe and veneration of religion amongſt men, then at other times in
the greateſt multitude; ſo is it the glory of
divine truth, that it can ſubſiſt by its own
proper evidence, and preſerve its ſtation in
the worſt of times, when all external arguments does moſt viſibly ceaſe.

Poſit.
V I.
     That its thus fully demonſtrable and clear,
how no ſimple inſtructing of men in the *ge-*
neral principles of religion, can be the proper
and adequate mean for ſuch a faith of aſſent
to the truth thereof, on its own evidence,
or

or anſwer that *Apoſtolick pattern of laying the foundation*, *Hebr.* 6: 2. but that ſome ſpecial duties elſe are called for to ſo high an end; ſuch wherein not only that true primitive confirmation in the Chriſtian faith might have ſome practical uſe, but we might alſo hope therewith, for a more remarkable out-letting of confirming influences of the Spirit of God. What is to be underſtood herein I ſhall humbly offer in a few *particulars*.

I. That it is one of the greateſt concerns of the *miniſterial worke*, and of the *key of doctrine*, to have all who heare the Goſpel, in the *Firſt* place preſſed to take religion ſo far to heart as to have a ſerious inquiry on the grounds and reaſons hereof, and thus to know their being on ſure ground herein, not becauſe they know not another way, but becauſe they know this is the alone way of truth, to which they dar truſt their immortal ſoul. II. That for this end the ſupreme truths of religion be repreſented with that certainty of *evidence, and demonſtration*, as both ſuch great and marvelous things does require, and the temper of ſuch a gainſaying age now calls for; and to have this preſſed more on mens judgment and conſcience, that the *things of God*, which are of the *higheſt conſequence, reality, and ſubſtance*, can have no poſſible reception by any implicit or probable

bable belief thereof, nor can admit any pretence for the fame, when the Lord hath given fuch kind of proofes and evidence, as
leaves mens darkneffe herein, without any
shaddow of excufe.

II. That it peculiarly belongs to the *Ca-
techetical work of religion* to take fome accompt of the meaneft profeffours thereof,
and with a fpecial refpect to the *youth*; of
their *faith of affent* to the doctrine of Chrift,
on what *grounds* and certainty of evidence
this is founded , and for their inftructing
therein, as well as in the *general principles* of
religion ; when one of the moft ruining
things to the Church lyes here, that the profeffion of moft is layed in fo deep an igno-
rance , as they have almoft nothing to fay
for the fame , but a naked affirmation. I
know the difficulty hereof for the weak may
be objected, but without juft caufe; fince
as the prime truths of religion are few, eafy
and plaine for the meaneft capacity, fo alfo
are the *primary evidences and demonftrations of
our faith*, if fuch once with that defire did
fearch after the fame as for a hid and invalua-
ble treafure; wherein this refpect should be
ftill had, to difference betwixt what is ini-
tial and of a more fundamental concern for
the weak, and what may tend to an higher
grouth and increafe of others.

III.

III. It should be of greatest use and advantage also for the same end, that the *young grouth* now coming up in the Church, were put to give some *explicit evidence* of their consent and choice of the profession of Christ, so far as may witnesse a ratification of the *baptismal covenant*, now as their own proper dead, wherein they were implicitly ingadged in their infancy. Some special grounds and reasons for this are; I. Becaufe God will have his service freely entered in and upon *choise*, as that way which is moft agreable to his honour; for as the *covenant* binds mutually, so doe the *feals* therof also, and therfor, upon our part is *baptifme a facremental oath of aledgence to God.* III. Becaufe it tends to a more refolute and firme adherence to the fervice of God, that this bufineffe should be perfonally brought home to mens confcience, efpecially before their firft admittance to the Sacrament of the Lords fupper, and thus to ingadg them as *Joshua* did *Chap.* 24: 22. *Ye are witneffes against yourfelves herein, and they faid we are witneffes.* III. Becaufe this is exprefly held forth 1 *Pet.* 3: 21. where *baptifme is called the anfwer of a good confcience toward God*, upon this ground, that fuch then who were come to years of knowledge, were perfonally fifted to confirme by their own confent that

folemne

folemne ingadgment and dedication by
Baptifme to be the Lords, and therefor it is
called ἐπερώτημα , which is *vox juris*, and
fignifies, *fponfio* , *& ftipulatio publica inter
Chriftianum*, *& Dominum Chriftum*, as the
moft judicious Commentators on that fcrip-
ture does clearly render; and fo this was a
fpecial part of the primitive practize , not
only with refpect to fuch, who were con-
verted from *Heathenifme*, but were born
within the Church and partakers of that *feal
of Baptifme in their infancy* , to fifte them
upon anfwer to that great demand of the
Covenant, doe yow now confent upon *evidence and choife* to be the Lords and to be a
fubject of his Kingdom, and embrace the
laws therof, and doe yow thus in fincerity
and truth declare the fame wherein you
have a good confcience before God. And
of what bleffed fruit and advantage should
this be both for the increafe and honour of
the Gofpel , if this were more deeply taken
to heart for fome practical ufe , according
to the *rule* , and *primitive pattern* in the
Churches of Chrift.

IV. It were fpecially defirable alfo , that
there be fome *clear view and fummary* by it
felf, of the moft *cogent grounds and demonftrations of the Chriftian faith*, with refpect
both to the *Doctrinal*, *Hiftorical*, and *Pro-
phetical.*

phetical part therof, and in that manner ac-commodate, as the meaneſt within the Church might have ſuch a help ſtill at their hand, and thus with the leaſt expenſe of time, be provided of ſuch arguments and reaſons, as should tend (through the bleſ-ſing of God) not only to the furtheſt ratio-nal aſſent, and certainty of the truth of their profeſſion, but to give a moſt ſpecial ſup-port of mind againſt that inward tryal of Sa-thans temptations and fiery darts this way; yea is ſuch a mean, that in the ſerious im-provment herof by having ſuch evidences once brought in on mens judgment and conſcience, ſo as to ſee with their own eyes the truth of the ſame, I muſt humbly judge, there is nothing, next to the internal work of the Spirit, of this kind might tend more to promote the Kingdom of Chriſt in this day.

   I ſhal but add this further on the preſent *poſit.* ſubject, that as there are ſome more *ſignal* V I I. *periods of time*, to which a greater brightneſſe and increaſe of light hath reſpect under the *New Teſtament*, ſo doth there now ſeem to be ſome remarkable call and excitment, to ſuch a *confirming work*, in this day about the Chriſtian faith; when we may hope that a more *ſolemne and reſtoring time of religion* in the world, is on a near approach, (though

all

all fenfible evidence would feem to control this) and may be now more looked after, then prepared for, under any fuitable impreffion of thefe *grounds* for the fame. I. That the promifed time of the *converfion of the Jewes* doth affuredly draw near ; and whatever be judged by fome of the Lords immediate appearence herein by a *miracle* , yet is it unqueftionable that nothing in the way of means could be more promifing and hopeful to promot this great end, then in promoting fo great a fervice as this for the Chriftian Church. II. That a greater extent alfo of the profeffion of Chrift amonghft the Gentils , and renting of the vaile that is now over many dark nations, feemeth clearly infured therwith ; and what a hopeful evidence fhould this be if fuch a *publick and catholick fpirit* were more feen, how to advance the higheft ends of religion on fuch an accompt without refpect to any partial or divided intereft ; yea that this bleft zeal of God might in that manner appear to have the dark world get a more clear and convincing profpect of the *higheft rational demonftrations of Chriftianity* , as might through the Lords gracious concurrence bring men once to an *inquifitive and ferious fpirit* about the fame. Oh that fuch may be thus raifed up in this difmal hower with

fome-

something of that ancient spirit , to travel
with desire for the *salvation of mankind*, and
of whom it may be said, as of blest *Nehe-
miah* , *these are indeed come to seek the wel-
fare of their people*, in their greatest interest.
III. And this farther excitment we are now
under for this end, in a time when Popery
seems to be upon one of its last and greatest
assaults against the Church; since its so clear
what ever tends to confirm men in Christianity from their own tryal and inquiry upon
the confirming evidences therof, must have
the same native result, to make such confirmed Protestants ; yea nothing is more demonstrable then that the method and
grounds that are taken both to ingadge and
fix men in the Popish profession, have the
same rational tendency to promot Atheism,
and to give infidels the greatest advantage to
reject the profession of Christ.

CHAPTER II.

*The confirming worke of Religion, reduced to
practical use; in some clear view of these
primary grounds, and demonstrations of
our faith; which none should pretend ig-
norance of, who enters the profession of
Christ upon choise, and certainty of evidence.*

SECTION I.

Qu. I. WHat *reasons*, and *demonstrations*, can yow give for so
great a faith of the *glorious being of God*,
when he is invisible to humane sense, since
this is the fundation of all religion?

ANSW. Though on the sacred truth
and authority of his own word, this is
principally founded, yet I am with the
furthest infallible *evidence* herein confirmed; I. That it can be no more sure,
this marvellous frame of the heavens and
earth hath a being, and is the object of
our sense, then that a supreme infinite wisdome and power must be the first cause
hereof, and it were simply impossible it
could ever otherwise have been. II. That
he hath thus made himself *visible* to our eyes
by such a *visible world*, and in so exquisite

an

an order and correspondence there to support the same, as nothing stands alone by
it self, but in a line of mutual respect, which
runs through the whole creation , whom
we may as clearly thus see, as that there is
an invisible soul in a living body. III. That
this harmony is amongst thinghs, in their
own nature so contrare and destructive to
other, for to hold this wonderful frame, as
all must abandon reason, or see an infinitly
wise conduct herein; and no need of extraordinary *miracles* , to confirme what the
whole constitutions of nature do witnesse. I V. That this rare frame of man could
never have come in being, but by him who
could unite such different substances as a
material body , and an *immaterial soul* , in so
near and marvelous an union. V. That
such an universal consent of mankind is in all
ages therto, as shews religion to be founded
in the very nature of man, and as essential
to his being, as his reason is; yea how the ultimate difference of man from the beast, and
most essential property of human nature lyes
here. VI. That though every one be an
enemy to what torments him ; yet was it
never possible for an Atheist to free himself
from that unavoidable sense and fear of a
Deity; nor, in a world so much lost in wickednesse, could ever extinguish the awe of
reli-

religion , or make any rational oppoſition to this greateſt article of the common faith of mankind. VII. That the reaſon of the whole conſtitution of nature , and viciſſitude of things here, is ſo great, as, without ſhutting out the uſe of reaſon, we cannot but ſee, how nothing poſſibly could have been better; and that any want hereof in the whole frame of the univerſe, would be as the diſlocation of a joynt of the body, and were not conceivable to be otherwiſe then it is by infinite wiſdome appointed. VIII. That its ſimply impoſſible that God bleſſed for ever ſhould not exiſt, or that this univerſe, (which is a worke ſo highly becoming the greatneſſe of its maker) could poſſibly ſubſiſt for one hour or minute of time, without a ſupreme independent power and being, on which all viſible beings have their dependance, ſince they cannot depend upon nothing. IX. That ſuch is the abſolute neceſſity of the *faith alſo of a God-head*, as without this the ſtate of mankind could not *morally* ſubſiſt, or any poſſible order, ſubjection, piety, and juſtice, be to ſupport human ſociety , but as *Bradwardine* ſaith, *O quam neceſſe eſt hunc eſſe, quem impoſſibile eſt non eſſe !* O that men cannot but ſee theſe effects of his power on the conſcience, in the certainty of a profetick light

and

as a rational being, more then the greateſt *monſter* in nature to be a true man.

Q u. I I. What doth witneſſe the *worlds* not being *eternal*, and its firſt original and beginning from God, to confirme your faith herein, by the further rational demonſtration.

A n s. I. That as an eternity is only communicable to the firſt cauſe, ſo that which is made up of corruptible & periſhing things, as this viſible world, cannot poſſibly be in it ſelf *eternal*; nor could ever produce it ſelf, ſince thus it muſt both exiſt and not exiſt at the ſame time, which is the greateſt contradiction. I I. That if there be ſuch a thing now *as time*, there can be no judging of dayes, yeares and ages to be infinite, or how one thing in a continued order, ſhould thus goe before another, without coming to ſome firſt beginning. I I I. If there be a gradual advance of human learning on the earth, and a further diſcovery of arts and ſciences; and that the greateſt experiments and inventions there have been but of a late riſe and date; then can there not poſſibly be an eternal ſucceſſion of mankind, with a

B 5   con-

continued progreſſe and experiency this way ; nor that but of late one part of the world is known and diſcovered to another. IV. That ſo ſhort an hiſtory as we have in the moſt ancient records of time , were wholly inconſiſtent with ſuch an eternal duration , or that infinite ages preceeding, ſhould leave no rememberance to poſterity, when ſo ſmall a meaſure of time , as a few *thouſand years*, have left ſo much. V. Nor could men beget other eternally without going back to ſome firſt man , who could not beget himſelf. VI. That if eternity be preferable to time, then ſhould not the excellenteſt being in the earth, *man*, be thus corruptible, and only this inanimate maſſe of the earth eternal. VII. That infinite ages paſt, though they ſhould have but multiplyed the race of man in an age , to two or three more, ſhould have come at laſt, that the whole precinct of the earth could not poſſibly bear the product of ſuch an infinite increaſe ; and no wears or extraordinary judgments were ever yet known to be ſuch, as to reſtrain ſuch an unavoidable grouth.

Qu.III. What infaillible evidence to reaſon is there of a *ſupream Providence*, both in the *conſervation, and government of the world*; for confirming your faith of the Scripture herein? .

ANSW.

ANS. I. That it is fo clear the fupport of this great frame of the Univerfe, with that continued & regular coure of nature herein, are as fimply impoffible without an infinite divine power, as its firft being and creation. I I. That fuch an extent of providence as refpeĉts fo innumerable objeĉts, with fuch a contrariety both of qualities and paffions in the fame, muft needs be from an infinite and intelligent caufe. I I I. That all things to this day, continue in that eftablished or- der of fecond caufes, wherein God hath pla- ced them by a law fo vifibly imprinted on the nature of things without reafon, that they doe as exaĉtly anfwer the fame in their proper courfe and ftation, as if they had a ra- tional knowledge of their duty. I V. That univerfal refpeĉt, the *fun in the firmament* hath to things here below, though at fo great a diftance, yet doth neither ceafe, nor weary to emit its beams and hid influences to the meaneft creatures, may let us clearly fee, how it hath the fame vifible ufe and end to confirme an incomprehenfible and infini- te providence about the meaneft things, as wel as the greateft. V. That immediate precedency of the foul in that leffer world of man, bears the fame evidence therwith, which though we never faw with our eyes, yet doth undenyably aĉtuate the whole bo- dy dy in its functions, as the proper spring of every act and motion there. VI. It is thus further confirmed, by these continued vicissitudes of *Summer and Winter*, and *of day and night*, that man might have, both light for his labour, and darknesse as a covering for his rest. VII. By such visible discoveries of *divine judgment and execution* of his laws on men here, as all may see his hand therin, who yet will not hear his voice in the word. VIII. By these extraordinare and wonderfull works of providence, which have been in all ages. IX. By so evident a restrainct both over *Devils*, *and wicked men*, without which they would quickly disturbe the whole frame of this earth, and make it uninhabitable for human society; if their being thus bounded and chained, were not as visible, as the certainty of their being. X. By such a *natural obligation* to moral duties, with the sense of a difference betwixt good and evil, as is founded in the very rational nature of man, that none can possibly root out, even where the Scripture is not known. XI. By that natural confidence also in God, and in a recourse to him on any present extreme hazard, to witnesse, not only the most high beares rule in the kingdomes of men, but that the sense and evidence hereof is unavoidable.

Qu.

Qu. IV. But doth this great *admini-*
ſtration of providence, about human affaires
as uncheangably appear, in a *differencing* betwixt the righteous and the wicked, by ſome
recompence to the one, and punishment to
the other, as in the eſtabliſhed courſe of nature.

Ans. It is ſure ſuch as deſire a confirming
of their faith herein, wants it not, with the
furtheſt evidence, but may ever ſee that
exact conformity in the whole diſpenſation
of providence, to the rectitude and perfection of the divine nature, and how a firm
beliefe *that God is*, and *that he is a revarder*
of them that diligently ſeek him, is one and the
ſame faith; when we cannot but ſee, I. That
natural ſenſe of good and evil, and eſſentiall
difference betwixt the ſame, which is ſo
fimly founded in the reaſon of all mankind,
as no human laws or cuſtome could ever take this off their conſcience, or make an indifference herin, without extinguiſhing the
very nature of man ; to ſhew that eternal
and uncheangable difference, which the holy nature of God hath put betwixt them.
II. That we ſee ſuch conſtraint ſerved
on the worſt of men, to an awful ſenſe and
regard of *truth and weal doing*, and to acknowledge the loveleneſſe and excellency
hereof, as does make them ſeek their own
re-

repute by a falfe shew and counterfite of the
fame; and gives fuch a being and rife to that
dreadful impofture of *hypocrify*. III. That
its the *truths* priviledge ever to outlive *fals-
hood* , and prevail over the fame, yea to
have the greater triumph after its foreft conflicts; and how this is of as foundamental a
conftitution in the courfe of providence , as
the moft firm eftablishment of nature.
IV. That in no time fince man was formed
in the earth , doth true *joy and ferenity of
mind* , ceafe to be the native refult of *weal-
doing* , or the *fruit of righteoufneffe , to be peace
and affurence of mind* , nor hath ever wanted a
witneffe even before the world of the Lords
taking pleafure herein.   V. That its fo evident, in the moft difmal times , what a publick *bleffing* , fuch are , who by more extraordinare tryals have been put to the higheft exercife of their grace and patience; yea
how vifibly fuch have been promot to the
moft honourable fervice for God , and to
advance the credite of religion before men ,
who on the firft fight and view have been
accounted the moft miferable of any.
VI. Whilft, *on the other hand* , it may be
ever feen , how with the greateft *profperity*
of the wicked here , there are *punishments of
another kind* difpenfed , and more dreadful
then any outward affliction, fuch as *judi-
sial*

cial obſtinacy, *and blindneſſe of mind in oppo-*
ſition to God, even when their own ruine is
made viſible to them herein.   VII. How
oft men are thus evidently condemned to be
happy in this world by ſome ſtrang meaſure
of *temporall ſucceſſe and proſperity*, before ſome great fall and ruine, as the iſſue hereof
in the laſt ſhene of providence doth fully at-
teſt. VIII. That its ſeen alſo, how ſin doth
ever bring its own *punishment* therewith, in
ſome begun degree both of ſhame and torment ; and, as *Seneca ,* an heathen could
ſay , *that wickedneſſe was the moſt exquiſite*
contriver of human miſery, ſo the world like-
wiſe may ſee how a preſent immunity from
judgment is no releaſe , but when its ſentence is not *ſpeadily execute* , yet is it at laſt ſurely execute.   IX. And how evident is it,
that the greateſt haters of godlineſſe are yet
inforced to juſtify the ſame and the Chriſtians choiſe herein, as the greateſt wiſdome,
upon any ſurpriſing ſtate and extremity ; yea
how ſuch would be glad to joyne intereſts
then with ſuch in their death , whom they
moſt contemned in their life.

Qu. V. How is it convincing and
demonſtrable, that God hath given any clear
and expres revelation of his will and councel
unto men , and that ſuch a *wonderfull record*
is undoubtedly extant in the world.

Answ,

Answ. That, I. it is not possible to believe the *being of God*, and not also the truth of an established *law*, and rule of commerce betwixt him and man here, so as to know both what we should doe, and what to expect and hope from him. II. That this also must be known and display its power and efficacy to the world, in that manner and by such infallible evidence of its truth, as may render all inexcusable, who give not intire credite therto. III. I can be no more clear and assured there is but one *sun in the firmament*, then that there is but one *fountain*, aud *repository of sacred light* about religion, which is the *Scripture*, and its being the alone publick standard of truth to the whole world. IV. That no way was ever made known to recover mankind from a state of bondage, darknesse, and misery, compatible with the very use of reason, but by this blessed light which shineth there. V. Yea that there is as visible a difference, betwixt the same and any pretended religion which ever was besides in the world, as there is *betwixt day and night*, which is founded in the immutable nature of these things in themselves. VI. That there is one proper *sphere*, where this glorious light of divine truth is fixed; and wherein it shines forth from one age to another; which is the Christian Church.   Qu.

Qu. VI. But what more peculiare evidences can yow shew of the *divinity of the Scriptures*, that all may fee to be of infallible truth.

Answ. I. That its fure fuch a *book* is this
day in the earth, which no created wisdome
could ever have done, and contains fuch
things of higheft conceirn to mankind, as
doe infinitly exceed the bounds of human
ability and invention, or could ever have
been difcovered but by God himfelf.
I I. That it gives forth fuch exquifite *laws*
and conftitutions of our religion, as men
muft needs fee the *holy nature, purity, and
perfection of God*, moft brightly shining forth
therin. III. Which doth difcover fo great
and proper a relief for all thefe evils and mi-
feries that doe attend this fallen eftate of
man, as none but an all fufficient God could
only doe. IV. That he alone muft be the
author of this bleffed record, who rules the
world, and hath determined the changes
and revolutions therof, when it is not more
evident how thefe vifible heavens are
ftretched forth over the earth, then that this
line of the Scripture is ftretched over the whole
worke and *frame of providence*, and doth
moft clearly illuminate the fame. V. That
furely this was the product of infinite wifdome, whence fo great a variety of matter,
doth meet with fo vifible a concent and har-

C   mony

mony in one perfect and intire frame ; yea
knit in fo cloffe a bond of union together,
as makes the whole Bible to be intirly *one
piece*; though in the writing of each diftinct
part therof it could never have poffibly been
contrived or forfeen by humane wifdome,
what we fee here of fo admirable an agree-
ment & correfpondence, as is in all the parts
therof. VI. That none els could have fpoke to
the world, in fo majeftick a way, & becoming
the greatneffe and foveraignity of God, to affume fuch a fupremacy, & give forth laws for
abfolute obedience from all mankind therto,
& on fuch a penalty of eternal deftruction; or
that any impoftures, either poffibly could, or
durft have, in fuch a manner, perfonate the
fame. VII. That it muft needs be his word
who perfectly knows what is in man, and
hath an abfolute authority over the foul,
and is a difcerner of the thoughts therof,
who thus not only gives law to the confcience, and our inward parts, but doth
eftablish an internal religion there, no leffe
abfolutly, then what refpects our external
worke and actions. VIII. Yea where all
may fee the whole penmen therof under fo
intire a fubjection to the doctrine which
they tought, and to be no contrivance of
their own, as they did record their own
failings, and imperfections in behalf of the
truth;

truth; and did thus alfo require all juft re-
fpe&t and obedience to the Magiftrates,
when through the whole earth they were
then greateft enemies to the truth of the
Gofpel. IX. That this muft be his word,
who alone can derive principles of life to his
own inftitutions, and animate the fame
with a quickning Spirit; and is a worke
above the contrivance of Angels or men,
when directed to each new tryal of the
Church, and perfonal cafe of Chriftians,
as though it had been alone writt for that
time; fo that I can be no more perfwaded in
reafon there is fuch a book as the *Bible* in the
earth, then that it came from heaven, and
is the alone rule of religion, and of divine
revelation, for the governing of mankind.

Qu. VII. How is the fecure *conveyance
of the Scripture* demonftrable amidft all the
changes of times paft, and that no poffible
acceffe could be for its corruption.

Answ. I. That its fo undenyably the
firft rule which ever was given to mankind
of religion, and the alone *publick ftandard
of truth*, that hath endured the tryal and inquiry of all times paft, fo as no pretences in
the matter of antiquity could yet ever be to
the contrare. II. That fo exact an *harmony*
is betwixt *the Old and New Teftament*, as
the one is a vifible tranfcript of the other, in

C 2   its

its accomplishment; that I can be no more
sure of such a venerable record as the Old
Teſtament, and its unalterable conveyance
to the Church, to which the whole race of
the Jewes is yet a ſtanding witneſſe, then
how it is continued and perfeſted in the revelation of the Goſpel, and but one intire
frame. III. That its deliverance was no
private deed, but by a publick truſt to the
whole univerſal Church; ſo as it were more
eaſy in the way of reaſon to queſtion the
moſt fundamental ſtatutes and lawes of any
nation, by which mens private right and
property is ſecured, then the truth hereof.
IV. That under the Goſpel it hath been ſo
fully diſperſed over the world, and in ſuch
various languages; as an innumerable company of Chriſtians theſe 1600 years paſt,
hath been as a common library of the ſame.
V. That theſe numerous verſions and com-
mentaries tranſmit theron in diverſe languages, doe fully evidence they had the ſame
Scripture, and no other then what we have
this day. VI. That this was delivered to
the Church not only in write, but in that
forme of ſound words, for keeping cloſſe
therby, as could admit no poſſible acceſſe
to corrupt or alter the ſame; beſides the continued and publick reference hath been ſince
the firſt ages of the Goſpel to its deciſion,
which

which all thefe sharpe controverfies , that have been in the Church on all fides , doe inevitably require.

Qu. VIII. What doth confirme the fall of man , and entry thus of fin into the world , this way , from clear and unavoidable evidences of reafon.

Answ. I. That there is fuch a thing as, fin and evil in the world, with the fenfe and confcience of guilt arifing hereon, amonghft all mankind, can need no proof or evidence. II. That it is fimply impoffible this should have been originally created with man, or effentially belonging to his firft frame and conftitution , fince then there could be no confcience of guilt or remorfe, for what was given to be a part of himfelf, in his firft frame; or be any fin, to act thus fuitably to their own original ftate. III. That it were not conceivable ,alfo how one part of *man* should be in fuch oppofition to another. IV. Nor that fuch a thing as *inherent shame* could be in the nature of man , upon the fence of *guilt*, and by fo natural a refult follow the fame, or that fuch should be ashamed of any part of his *own being*, if this were not upon ane undoubted *apoftacy* from what once he was, and that inevitable conviction of confcience that he now is what he ought not to be, fo as the certainty of *mans fall*

C 3   though

though alone revealed in the Scripture, as to
the true cause thereof, yet may be as evident.
to *reason*, as the truth of his being now is.

SECTION II.

Qu. I. **A**Re there such *assistances* to the
Christian faith upon that great
and astonishing mystery of the revelation of
Christ to the world as can fully answer the
greatnesse thereof from cleare and infallible evidence to mens judgement?

Answ. It is sure there could nothing possibly be desired more to satisfy the most
doubtfull and suspicious minde then is given
for the furthest certainty hereof. I. That
such *a glorious person* as the *Messiah* was to
come, and be *anoynted* to that great work
of *redeeming mankinde* from sin and misery
and bring man back again unto God; and
how this *promise* is the alone foundation,
whereon the *church* was founded since man
fell. II. That all these numerous *types and
sacrifices* under the *law*, did so expresly tend
to confirm their faith of that one blessed
propitiatory sacrifice which was to be offered
up. III. That long er the *New Testament*
was writ, there was so cleare and exact a
portraicture of the *Messias* drawn forth in
the *old*, with such peculiar marks whereby
he

he should be knowen to the *church*, and have infallibly taken place in the event as men could not upon any *Scripture evidence* exſpect his comming in another way. IV. That his *humiliation and ſufferings* were ſo expreſly shewed forth and foretold, with the peculiar circumſtances thereof in the 53. *chap. of Iſaiah*, and 9. *of Daniel*, as if they had been eye wittneſſes of the accomplishment thereof. V. That even the ſpeciall *ſeaſon* and period of time for outmaking of this *great promiſe* was ſo far made knowen, as upon diligent ſearch and inquiry, its neare approach might be diſcernable and cleare to *what or what manner of time* this did ſpecially relate; for which both the *fall of the monarchies* and *Daniels ſeventy weekes* were ſet up as highway markes to guide mens faith herein. VI. That its ſimply impoſſible according to the Scripture, how the promiſed *Meſſias* could be yet to come, except the *Jewes* were put in the ſame ſtate they were in at his coming, when now for theſe 1600. Jeares there hath been no *Scepter*, nor *lawgiver*, no *temple*, or *daily Sacrifice*. VII. That this great myſtery could never poſſibly have entered in our thoughts, or be deviſed by any created underſtanding.

Qu. II. But are there as cleare and infallible evidences of the truth of this great

promiſe

promise in the event, that surely the blessed *Messias* of the world is now come, as that it is sure he was promised.

ANSW. Its beyond all possible debate. I. That so *divine and wonderfull a person* was in the dayes of *Tiberius Cæsar* manifested then to *Israel*, with no outward shew or observation; who did so great and marvellous things, before all the people, as were above all created power, yea, was *crucifyed at Jerusalem*, under *Pontius Pilate*, and is a truth in the matter of fact, that both Jewes and heathens have been enforced to confesse. II. That this special season of his comming into the world as the *great Epocha* and period of time from which the *Christian church*, hath since to this day reckoned her state and succession, is undoubted and clear also. III. That the time of his appearance unto the world, did so exactly tryst with that which was foretold by the *Prophets*, as then the *Jewish church* was with greatest advertance looking after the *Messias*; so as some remarkable *impostors* were thus excited to deceive the people herein. IV. That in him who was then revealed, and whom the Christian church *worships* its sure, was most exactly fulfilled, what ever was foretold, concerning the Messias in the Old Testament; and we do appeal herein to these *records*

cords which all the *Jewes* even to this day do acknowledge to be divine. V. That this was not done in a corner, but in the publick view of men in these dayes, most noture and famous; yea by the special destination of God at so solemn a time of the *passover in Jerusalem*, where *Christ* our *passover was then sacrificed*. VI. That no humane interest or policy can possibly be in this discovery of the *gospell*; when nothing more visibly crosse therto or obstructive of its successe, then such a publishing of the *death and sufferings of our Lord*, with all the ignominy and abasement which attended the same, had there been any accesse here to consult carnal reason, or any other ground to beare it out then the evidence and certainty of its truth. VII. That herein have all divided partyes *and sects* in the Christian world been enforced stil to meet and consent, in ane acknowledgement of the substance thereof. VIII. That in the same light which was held forth in the Old Testament about the *Messias*, did the whole *gentile church* enter; and made claime to their right for being adopted the seed and children of Abraham, on these cleare and expresse promises given for the same; which the Jewes could not but confesse to be of divine authority.

    Qu. III. What confirmation

Christian

Chriſtian faith, that for 4000. yeares the
comming of the Meſſias should be deferred
after the promiſe.

· A n s. Though the ſoveraign pleaſure of
God should ſilence and ſatisfy our minde
herein; yet is there ſuch a ſight to be had
hereof, and of infinit divine wiſedome
shining forth in the ſame as should be moſt
confirming for theſe *ends.* I. That there
might be a more diſtinct repreſenting of the
glory of this myſtery to angels and men, in ſuch
a graduall opening up of the ſame. II. To
put that weight and high value on his own
promiſe and teſtimony herein, when on the
alone credit thereof, he would thus both
try, and beare out the *faith of his church,*
for ſo many *ages,* and draw forth their deſires and longings in all that long ſpace of time
after the ſame. III. To teſtify the greatneſſe
of his wrath againſt *ſin* and the *Apoſtacy of
mankinde,* by ſuffering the generality thereof to ly ſo long under its *fatall* effects. IV.
To prepare the *church* for ſo *great a reception,*
by all that long *preparatory ſervice of legall
inſtitutions,* as ſo highly becoming the greatneſſe of this *myſtery,* to have ſo ſolemn and
ſtupendious ane introduction thereto. V.
That thus the world might have its full tryall
of the inſufficiency of natural abilityes, and
of any improvements of humane wiſedome
and

and learning, for help; after this had firſt
been at the furtheſt hight both in *Greece and
Rome*, before the alone *Redeemer* of the
church came.

Q u. I V. What can offer furtheſt conviction to the world of the truth of Chriſtianity from its nature and internall excellencies; and that it is no leſſe eſſentially good
in its ſelfe, then evidently true.

Ans. I. That its ſo undeniable even to theſe
that live at a diſtance, how ſuch is the *truth
of Chriſt* that though all viſible and humane
props ſhould faill, it can ſubſiſt by its *own
evidence, and authority* over mens conſcience,
and hath thus ever preſerved its ſtation in
the worſt of times. I I. That as it holds
forth the moſt exquiſite *rule of perfection* to
follow, ſo doth bring the greateſt releef to
the diſtempers of the minde, and theſe mi-
ſeries which attend humane ſtate here; ſo
as a higher glory doth thus reſult to the *holy
God*, by this *diſpenſation of Grace* to fallen
man then if he had ſtood in his *primitive ſtate.*
I I I. That it is ſure the truth and doctrine of
Chriſt doth natively tend to fix men in a
ſtate of light and communion with God, and in
a *ſtate of ſeparation* of ſuch in their *principles,
affection*, and *converſation* from the world.
I V. That it doth more brightly ſhine forth
in *ſimplicity, and truth and in its internall* and

and vitall acts, then in any outward form or shew, yea in the way of *selfe deniall*, *meek-neffe*, and *poverty of spirit*, doth such ane excellency appeare, as in *its oun nature*, hath as visible a difference from the proud and vindictive spirit of this world, as the *day* hath from the *night*. V. How such is *Chriftianity*, as by no naked *doctrinall* difcovery of the fame, to mens judgement, or such rules as any humane fcience is acquired by, can be knowen, without ane inward power and principles of a *new life*; nor can there ever be a right knowledge of *divinity*, untill it be firft ingrafted in a *divine heart*; fo far is this *myftery* above all humane rule, and contrivance. VI. That it is ftated in the greateft oppofition to any falfe shew or *hypocrify*; yea, brings fuch inforcements therewith of candor, and truth, and of *love*, *tenderneffe and fympathy* towards others, as all muft fee is not only the higheft ornament and perfection of our nature, but the greateft *bleffing to the world* that ever was knowen. VII. That fuch a native *luftre and fragrancy* doth attend the truth, and fimplicity of the gofpell, as its no more poffible for humane *art* or cunning to reprefent this, then to make the dead image of a *man* to live, or to paint in a broad the *vitall fcent* of a violet or rofe, to our *fenfes*. VIII. That in this way

of

of the *gospels* subduing men to the obedience
thereof, by the power of *inward grace*, the
glory of Christ doth more eminently shine
forth, then if he had appeared for this end
with the greatest outward majesty and atten-
dance of Angels to our bodily eyes. IX.
That it is so visible how the whole world
besides, that is without the revelation of
Christ, is a place where horrour, falsehood,
and impiety doth manifestly reign.

Qu. V. But how do yow receive so
wonderfull a truth, as that of the Gospell is,
when its now so great a distance of time from
its first promulgation.

Ans. I. That we can be no more sure
and perswaded of the most visible and present objects of sense, then, that this is the
same *gospell* which is still shining forth to the
world, whereby ane innumerable company
of all *nations*, *tongues* and *languages*, hath
received the *spirit*, and been *sealed*; yea,
hath made that change upon men, in turning
them from *ungodlynesse and idols to serve the
living God*, as hath been no lesse marvellous
then the turning of so many *wolves*, into
lambs. II. That it is the same *gospell* which
not only through a series of 16. *centuries*
hath been attested, but by such innumerable
witnesses who counted not their life deare
unto the death for sealing thereof, and found

it

it fweet to be offered up in the flames for *Chrift*. III. Which in all ages paft hath ftood out the greateft oppofition that ever the world made to any intereft, while the *weapons of its warfare were spiritual, and not carnal;* & with that fucceffe as the time of the *Churches hotteft perfecution* from heathens was that period of time alfo of a moft remarkable fpreading in the world. IV. That the fame *Gofpel* is revealed this day, which hath had fuch difcernable *triumphs* and fucceffe when no external affiftance could be feen herein; and no vifible power by which it gained the moft favage and dark parts of the earth, to take on the *yoak of Chrift*, and prefer the objects of faith to the moft defireable *objects of fenfe.* V. Yea, which hath not only had fuch *vital influence* on mens heart, and practice to change it into the fame *image*; but that herein the doctrine of the *croffe of Chrift* in the greateft *fimplicity* hath ftill been the moft effectual way of its conqueft, and the greateft attractive on mens fouls to receive the fame.

Qu. VI. How is it demonftrable that fuch remarkable fufferings of times paft for the truth of Chrift, were both founded on the alone certainty thereof, and carryed out by a divine Spirit above any affiftance of nature.

ANSW.

Answ. That it is sure, I. Here was no *comedy*, or perfonated fufferings which the *primitive Chriftians*, and in after times did endure for *Chrift*; or that thefe unexpreffable torments and paines were any *dream*, and *delufion* either to themfelves or the world, and that their adverfaries did thus conflict and wreftle with their own *shadow* in fo continued and cruel ane oppofition. II. That fuch *joy and exultation of Spirit* thefe witneffed amidft their *torments*, who otherwife wanted no fenfe or feeling of their paines and fufferings, could have no rife but what was fupernatural. III. That this could be no poffible diffimulation or *counterfit* when they were ftepping in on *eternity*, nor the product of a diftempered judgment; whilft all might fee what ferioufneffe of Spirit, *tenderneffe*, *and bowels of compaffion* to their adverfaries they did then evidence. IV. That thefe greateft fufferings were upon choife, and to endure rather then to be fafe at the rate of receding in any thing from the truth. V. Yea no natural reafon can comprehend how fuch mean and feeble perfons as many of thefe were, should endure, what would have made the greateft *natural courage* to faint, as if they had foregone humane paffions which flesh and blood muft needs have herein, fo as I am conftraind to fee fomething

no

no lefs marvellous and fupernatural in the
faith of martyres, then in the *faith of miracles*.

SECTION III.

Q u. I. **I**S it fully demonftrable, · that the
faith of a deity, and of fuch an
eftablifhment as a religious worfhip, muft
neceffarly determine men to be *Chriftians*,
on this ground that they cannot but fee how
religion hath not another being in the earth,
but in the truth of *Chriftianity*.

Answ. It is fimply impoffible to make a
rational tryal herin, and not fee the certainty of this demonftration, to be thus
clear. I. That there needs no more for
any of a ferious fpirit, but to come and fee,
what the whole frame of *Heathenifme* was,
and if it be poffible to deny, even under
any fenfe of the law and dictates of nature,
its being the higheft reproach of mankind;
and how the very *myfteries* of that *Heathenifh
worfhip*, was fo horrid and impure, as they
needed a vail then from the common view
of the world. I I. Nor can there be a rational reflection this day, on that ftrang mon-
fter of *Mahumitanifme*, but of a vifible *pro-
digy* of the judgment of God, on thefe parts
of the earth; upon their apoftacy from the
Chriftian faith, by giving men up to fuch an
impofture,

impofture, as expofeth the very name and form of religion, to derifion; and can never claime a reception either from the purity of its rule or internal evidence of the truth therof, or of its having any poffible confiftence with it felf. III. That its fure alfo the *Jewish religion* had never another being but in the truth and faith of *Chriftianity*, and where this fundation is divided from, it hath none at all; yea how that people unto this day are fuch a confirming witneffe to the Chriftian Religion, as its ftrang this doth not beget deeper impreffions on mens fpirit. So that there is an abfolute neceffity, we muft either forgoe the ufe of reafon, or fee, if there were not fuch a rule given and revealed for commerce betwixt God and man, as the *Scripture*, where the laws and conftitutions of the *Chriftian faith*, are for this end held forth, that its then fure there is no fuch thing, as any religion in the earth, but what wer fo highly irrational and abfurd, as fhould rather juftify *Atheifm*.

Qu. II. What fpecial confirmation to *Chriftianity*, can this vifible ftate of the *Jews* bear, who are in fo expreffe an oppofition to the Gofpel of Chrift?

Answ. If this were brought near our thoughts we fhould find it one of the great affiftances to our *faith*. I. That its fure there

D   is

is fuch a people and race, as a living and vifible evidence to our fenfe, of the truth of
that renowned *nation, and church of Ifrael*,
to which the *oracles of God* were committed,
and thus are ftill, as fome part of the evident
ruines of that once flourifhing ftate. II.
That the world may fee, fuch a people kept
by themfelves and not mixed with the nations, whofe fathers from one generation
to another did ftill own the *divinity of the
Old Teftament*; and doth atteft that doctrine, in which the truth and fubftance of
Chriftianity lyes, even whilft with greateft
malice they oppofe the Chriftian faith, to
witneffe there can be no poffible collufion
here. III. Their being under a ftroak of
that *judicial* induration and blindneffe of
mind, as no reafon could poffibly comprehend fuch a thing, how they fee not the light
in the very noon-day of the Gofpel, if it
were not exprefly fortold their being concluded under fuch an arreft of judgment,
until the *fulneffe of the gentiles* be brought in.
IV. That fo immediate an appearence of
God, is in the *judgment* of that people,
both in the manner and continuance thereof, as no inftance could ever be found to
refemble the fame, fince man was formed
in the earth; and thus as a confpicuous mo-
nument of divin wrath, fet up for every
age.

age and time of the Church, to turn aſide and conſider this great ſight, and inquire what means ſo ſtrang and amazing a thing, as the *ſtate* of the *ſcattered Jews* is, now under the times of the Goſpel. V. That this deſolation on them and ſtroak, had ſuch ſpecial concurring circumſtances for giving light therto; as being not above 48 *years*, *after the death of Chriſt*, with their hands, as it were, hot and reaking with that *blood* which they had wiſhed on them, and their children; that it ſhould be at that time of the *Paſſover*, which was the very ſame of the *ſufferings of our bleſſed Lord* there, and pointing as with the *finger* at the ſame; as alſo by the *Romans*, whoſe intereſt in their oppoſition to Chriſt they pretended to own.

Qu. III. Is the *way and manner* of the *Goſpels promulgation* ſuch, as no other profeſſion could ever pretend to, and where all may ſee there can be no human intereſt or contrivance in the ſame?

Answ. It is undenyable, that no intereſt elſe was ever in ſuch a way promot and does exceed all natural underſtanding, how the truth of Chriſtianity could in this manner prevail. I. To perſwade men without any *motives*, or inducements from this preſent world, to imbrace a doctrine ſo wholly repugnant to nature; yea to preferr an intereſt

of things *not seen*, and which none ever in
the earth faw, to the moſt deſirable *objects
of ſenſe*.   II. To admit no *implicit reception*
from any, but on their exacteſt inquiry and
tryal herein ; or in an other way claime an
intereſt in mens affections, but by a full aſſent of their light and judgment to the ſame.
III. To admit no gratification to the moſt
predominant deſires and inclinations of men
upon any darling ſin, which according to
human wiſdome would be judged of an abſolute neceſſity for gaining any acceptance
with ſuch ; yea to give no partial reſpect to
the greateſt *Princes* more then to the meaneſt.
IV. To purſue its intereſt, by ſo plain a
diſcovery of the *death*, *and ſufferings of our
bleſſed Lord*, *with the whole ignominy thereof*,
when nothing could more evidently control ſuch an end by any rules of human wiſdome and policy, if there had been a poſſible acceſſe to conſult fleſh and blood herein.
V. And its ſure there could be no deſigne,
without an immediate divine power, in ſuch
a manner to plead the intereſt of Chriſtianity with men, by inſerting affliction, and
the *croſſe* in the firſt entry, as *eſſential to the
profeſſion thereof*, and holding forth the
neceſſity of taking on the *yoke of Chriſt*,
without which none can be his *Diſci-
ples*.

Qu. IV.

Qu. IV. But wherein doth the evidence of that great demonstration of the Gospel most clearly appear, in the *love and unity of Christians* amonghst themselves, which we find Christ doth so specially presse, for this end, that the world might know, and have such a visible seal of his *divine mission*, *Joh.* 17: 21.

Answ. The greatnesse of this demonstration may be thus evident to all. I. That its so clearly demonstrative of the *purity of our Religion*, which can admitt of no bitternesse, strife, recrimination, or such indecencies of heat and passion, which are these fatal effects of discord in the Church; and thus lets us see the excellency of the *spirit and rule* of the Gospel. II. That thus also we may know the power and efficacy of the truth thereof, *which is according to godlinesse;* upon mens heart, in subduing these distempers of the mind and judgment. III. That this doth so specially tend to make religion *lovely*, and to draw forth matter of praise and blessing to God from the world, when they see such a native effect of Christianity as this, to make those who professe the same in that manner shine forth in *tendernesse, humility,* and *brotherly love*, so that they become as a publick good and blessing to mankind in the place they are in. IV. This ap-

pears

pears also from the nature of that *union in the Church of Christ*, and amonghst his followers, which only a divine power could both frame and make effectual; and its sure no human society or constitution could ever claim such an *unity* therein as this is ; where not only persons of all nations and languages and of all conditions, both high and low, but of the most different interests, humours, and dividing circumstances in other things, doe yet in so marvelous an *harmony* meet in the *body of Christ which is his Church* here in the earth.   V. Because herein also doth the glory and honour of our *blessed head*, more eminently appear in securing this *unity* of his Church, under a *diversity of light* and judgement otherwayes, by a spirit of love, meeknesse and condescendence amongst his people; then by imposing the most severe and absolute uniformity in all things, to be the alone condition of *Christian communion*.

Qu. V. But what strength and evidence doth this *demonstration* of the Gospel, now bear in so *divided a state* of religion, and when the wounds and breaches of the Church this day are like to blood unto death?

Answ. Whatever just cause be of griefe, yet is there none for darkening the truth of this *demonstration*, on these grounds. I. That none can deny the perfection of the *rule* of the Gospel, for the most firm and intire unity amonghst all the followers of Christ on the earth. II. That no opposition which is made therto, but what hath been *fortold* as one of the greatest tryals of the Church under the *New Teſtament*, and the Spirit of God doth most expreſly point at in theſe *latter times*. III. Becauſe the furtheſt *oppoſition* thereto can be no more cauſe for any to ſtumble, or queſtion the truth of this *demonſtration*, then that there is a *Devil*, whoſe greateſt deſigne hath ever been to divide and break Chriſtians amongſt themſelves. IV. Becauſe this *union*, which is chiefly *miſtical and inviſible*, is much greater oft, then what this way may appear to the world, and of that kind as is not interrupted by diſtance of place, or any want of local communion. V. That ſuch a *guard* is ſet by the Lord unto this piece of his glory, and to oppoſe any invaſion thereon; that there ſtands an *Angel with a flaming ſword*, upon every hand in the *commands* and *threatings* of the Goſpel, to ſecure this bleſſed *unity* of the Saints amonghſt themſelves, ſo as none can invade the ſame but on their higheſt peril, of oppoſing that which is as the *apple of Chriſts eye*. VI. That its ever found how this demonſtration hath ſome clear evi-

dence

dence amonghft fuch who are indeed the
Difciples of Chrift, and according to their advance in the life and power of Chriftianity
doth the more brightly shine forth; fo that
the nearer the *lines* are to the *center* , the
nearer alfo are they amonghft themfelves.
VII. That in all times there hath been fome
tremenduous *marke* of the judgment of God
made vifible on fuch who are *contentious,* and
have made it their worke to *caufe divifion* in
the Church and fow difcord among brethren.

Qu. VI. But what hath the Church
now in thefe latter dayes to compenfe the
want of that great demonftration by *miracles* , and fuch extraordinare confirmations
of the Chriftian faith , as were in the firft
times?

Answ. I. That we may fee how far that
feal of martyrdome , which came in the
roome of *miracles* to the Church, hath exceeded that which was in the firft times of
the Gofpel. II. That there hath been fince
fuch innumberable *shining examples of holineffe* , yea thefe continued to this day,
whom the world might fee did walk in the
light and power of Chriftianity, as fure as
men walks, under the power and vertue of
a living foul. III. That we now fee what a
length the *courfe* of the Gofpel and of the
.Church

Church militant is come, and how far thus the *times of the Gentiles are fulfilled*, which once was so contrare to all human appearence. IV. That so sure and exact *a performance of the Scripture*, is now undenyable in the event, and of such great and marvelous things which were fortold under the *New Testament*, that in an ordinare way none could have believed, what we see with our eyes, and now have these things, which were in former ages the *object of the Churches faith*, made the *object of our sense*; and its sure this is such *a seal* and confirmation to our faith in these last times as doth much exceed the greatest *miracles* which were with the *first planting of the Gospel*. V. Though we may not resolve our faith on any *extraordinare providences*, or lay the least weight hereon to support the authority of the doctrine we professe, since this only is founded on that sacred revelation of *divine truth in the Scripture*, which is that infallible rule to discerne true miracles, and what is Gods seal herein under the undoubted signature and stampe of his own power and working in the same; yet hath there been such incontrollable evidence of extraordinare signs and confirmations to confirme the truth of the Reformed Religion, since the Reformation, as in no ages past was ever known,

but

but with the firſt planting of the Goſpel
among the Gentiles.

' SECTION IV. '

Qu. I. **I**S it cleare and demonſtrable that
the *doctrine of Chriſt* , is a *ſoull
quickening* and *experimental religion* , and the
trial thereof, in its moſt ſupernatural truths,
of ſuch rational certitude and evidence, as
the world can no more deny or queſtion the
ſame then theſe *experiments of nature*, that
are of moſt univerſal uſe?

Answ. Though men looked but at a
diſtance here or were come from *Heathniſm*,
ſo for as to make a ſerious trial of *Chriſtianity*,
its ſure they could not but ſee, and be fully
perſwaded in their judgement, hereof on
theſe grounds. I. That ſuch a diſcovery is
undoubted and cleare in the *Scripture* of ſo
great things, as, that there is *a holy Ghoſt*,
and his workings on mens ſouls, of *peace with
God*, and the *joy of his preſence*, which all
who receive the goſpel are called to know
and prove on their oun trial. II. That this
wittneſſe of Chriſtian *experience*, hath as
diſcernable a conſent and harmony there
with as face anſwereth to face in the glaſſe,
and is cleare to be no *caſual thing*, but where
every ſtep in this way of *trial*, is by *Scripture
light*

light , and what they did before read there , ere they knew it on their oun foul. III. That this in all ages of the *church* and wherever fuch as ferved God in the fpirit were found in the moft *remote parts* from others , hath ftill been the fame; and like a *great roll* is tranfmit from one generation to another , with their *confirmatory feal, that God is faith-full and true* , in thefe truths of his word which feem moft incredible to the world, & now comes to our hand to require the fame atteftation and wittneffe. IV. That thefe who know and teftify thefe things once found it not eafy to beleeve the fame and did no leffe judge of fuch *great experiments of religion* as a dream or imaginary thing then moft now doe, until they knew them on their foul. V. That fuch alfo have been the moft *burning and shining lights* that ever were in the church and thefe innumerable in all ages who declare the fame , yea this in the mouth of the grave and entran e to ane eternal ftate when no outward intreft could fway them here. VI. That it muft be a matter of greateft affurance which hath then preffed the moft tender *parents* with their laft and dying breath to commend the fame *trial to their children* , and to obteft their making earneft herein as the greateft intereft they could leave them. VII. That what ever

diffe-

differences be oft among thefe in fome matters
of truth : yet, in the certainty of this great
trial of the life, power and comforts of religion, is ane *harmonious onenes* in the fame
teftimony in all times of the church. VIII.
That if any queftion this becaufe fo remote
from mens *fenfes*, and the judgement of carnal reafon; the reality of its *effects*, doth
unanfwerably prove both the *reality* and
excellency of the caufe.

Qu. II. What cleare and rational conviction can yow offer, of fo great a thing as
converfion of men from a ftate of nature, to a
new ftate by grace, which doth raife them as
far above the refidue of mankinde, as reafon doth above the ftate of the beaftes?

Answ. Though I should ftrive againft the
conviction of fuch a *miracle*, and demonftration of the Gofpel, as *converfion* is, yet
were it not poffible to deny fuch demonftrative evidences as the world cannot but fee
hereof. I. That it is fure fuch a *change* is made
effentially requifite to the *being*, and conftitution of a Chriftian, by the whole confent
of the Scripture. II. That there was never
yet ane *argument in nature*, for ones being a
Chriftian in the life and power thereof what
ever may be for a naked form or shew. III.
That they are not a *few*, but innumerable
inftances in all times and of all rancks & conditions

ditions of men on whom so great a *change* and difference hath been made thus evident, both from themselves what once they were, and from the residue of the world. IV. That this hath been not only upon such as have been *signally impious* in their practise, but who in their judgment were wont to deread holynesse as a fancy, so as *Atheists* must grant that there have been as profest *Atheists* sometimes as themselves, who have been made such conspicuous monuments of the power of the gospel. V. That none can object here, as once the *Jewes* did, doe any of the *rulers*, or such as the world counts most *wise*, and knowing stand wittnesses to the same ; when it is so knowen there have not been more *wise*, *learned*, and *judicious* in the things of reason upon the earth, then such as have been eminent examples of the power of conversion. VI. That its marvellous *effects* in subduing men, to what once was there predominant interest and idol, and to part from what had been as their *right eye*, *or hand* could only be from ane immediat divine power. VII. That such as were greatest adversaryes to the truth, have been made no lesse eminent *instruments* in the service of Christ, and choise vessels of honour, then once they were in their enmity and opposition. VIII. That this change hath

been

been fo difcernable in times of moft vifible
perfecutions and hazard, when no outward
advantage or gaine could have the leaft influence thereon. Now as thefe are demonftrably cleare, fo can there be no poffible acceffe to queftion this. I. That the *Scripture*
is faithfull and true in fo great a difcovery.
I I. That there is a *divine fpirit* and a power
above nature, which accompanyes the fame
in fuch a change. I I I. That there are furely,
contrary ftates in ane other world, when they
are fo undeniably manifeft here.

Qu. I I I. But can fo great ane experiment of religion as that of *communion betwixt
God and men*, here upon earth be made ratio-
nally convinceing to fuch as are themfelves
ftrangers thereto; and for a further confirming of the Chriftian faith?

Answ. Though this be ane *experiment* of
divine truth of a more tranfcendent intereft
and value then all that ever were in nature,
yet is it no leffe *evident*, there can be no poffible delufion herein; if I. to which fo *innumerable a company* beares teftimony and
hath tranfmit the fame, as that which not
once or twice they have proven but in the
continued trial of their life. I I. That its
known to the world, how fuch as teftify
what they doe, and have fo oft found in the
retirement of their fouls with God, are of as

difcer-

discerning spirits to know the true value of things, as any elfe; yea fuch whofe teftimony in other things the worft of men could not refufe nor deny. III. How its undeniably evident, fuch muft know ane other acquaintance and *fociety then that of men;* that not only makes thefe hid exercifes of godlines fo defireable, where all may fee they more flee then follow any humane wittnefle, but thus makes fo vifible a change oft both in their cafe and countenance after moft fad anguifh and dounecaftings of fpirit. IV. That it is fo evident alfo how fuch as are moft ferious this way, have been vifibly oft raifed above their ordinary cafe, and frame in prayer, and other dutyes of religion; yea, in that manner, as they who never knew, there is a *holy Ghoft* but by report, could not withftand fo cleare conviction of the reality hereof, that can beget fuch *liberty*, *humble tendernefle* and melting of heart, yea fuch difcernable joy and confidence. V. That no delufion or falfe fhew can be here, when its ever feen, how fuch as are moft ferious and frequent in *prayer* and thefe hid retirements with God, are the moft flourifhing alfo in the *vitals* of Chriftianity, and have the moft honorable luftre, and appearance of any in their profeffion. VI. That its fuch only whofe joy and comfort is moft fpecially

difcer-

difcernable beyond others when thefe lower
fprings of outward help and encouragement
are moft vifibly fhut up.

Qv. IV. Is that great, and experimental
part of religion in the *power of the confcience*
over man, fuch as may be as demonftrable
to the world, as the truth of a rational
being?

Answ. It may be matter of wonder how
men are not ftruck with deeper convictions
hereon, when they cannot but fee. I. That
though this be the greateft *tormentor*, and
troubler of the world, yet is there no poffible retreat from its power tho they fhould
flee to the uttermoft parts of the earth, but
doth thus enforce the foul to a *reflexion on its
felfe* even when it trembleth at that fight.
II. Which caufeth fuch feare and horrour
upon the commitment of *fecret fins*, when
no dread of humane wittneffe, or of vifible
hazard this way could ever occafion this.
III. Which admits no violence in any to
outdare the fame, but is a power that the
greateft monarches finde to be ftronger then
they; and is fuch, as thefe oft are enforced
for a prefent eafe, and releefe either to divert,
or bribe the fame by fome falfe grounds of
peace. IV. That it conftraines men to
juftify God, and *judge themfelves* when his
hand doth purfue them, and to finde out
their

nd guilt, which was before hid,
makes men alfo afrayed to be alo-
mfelves; and to tremble at the
th, becaufe its *light doth torment*
hat unavoidable application the
nakes hereof. VI. Yea makes
ɔ legible oft in their countenan-
hen they ftudy moft to conceale
y fee, there is ane accufer with-
thority and power cannot poffi-
ned. VII. Which with fo re-
onfidence, and *fecurity* doth fup-
pirit and makes it eafy to fuftain
nfirmityes from without, when
; yea, thus upholds the oppreft
kable peace and comfort, when
aufe the oppreffours to tremble.
But what doth moft neceffarly
fo cleare a demonftration as the
for confirming of our faith?
I. That its infallibly thus cleare,
s a *higher power* and *judgment*, to
ankinde is fubjected, & gives the
ɩavoidable demonftration, both
; of *God*, & the *truth of his word*,
& fupernatural difcovery which
reof. II. That there is a fupream
law alfo & invifible judge above
whofe power and authority this
ice doth without refpect of per-

E   fons

fons both *ſummond*, *arreſt*, bring in *wit-neſſe* and *ſentence* great and ſmall. III. That the *internal government* of our *bleſſed Lord*, this way both in the ſeverity of his rebukes and moſt ſenſible enlargements of peace and comfort is unavoydably demonſtrat. IV. That it beares ſo clear evidence to that unknowen and undoubted *releef*; and how none elſe could be ever found, to theſe wounds and ſtings of the conſcience, but in the *light and power of Chriſtianity*. V. That it is ſimply impoſſible for men to delight freely in a courſe of ſin, when no humane power can diſarm the conſcience of that ſo intollerable *a ſting*, by which it begins ſo early a hell within the ſoul. VI. That ſuch is the power and peace of a good conſcience as can make it ſtand unbroken. amidſt the greateſt ruines and terrours of the world when under ſuch a guard, as it is wrapped up in its own *innocency*.

SECTION V.

Qu. I. IS the evidence of a *Kingdome of darknes*, in a direct oppoſition and contrariety, to that Kingdome of light, which Chriſt hath ſet up by the Goſpel, ſuch as the certainty thereof may be a matter of ſenſe, as well as of faith?

ANSW,

ince this is of such special use,
rm the christian faith and awa-
deeper reflexion on the same,
ere seemes no accesse to deall,
from *palpable experience* ; it is
deny. I. That there is such
he *devil* and these *wicked spirits*
the earth , yea that have ane
amiliar converse with many
That these spirits though once
:ellent , have fallen into such
, as all may see their aim and
, is to *dishonour God*, and des-
in man. III. That it is im-
ny the *marks* of that power and
hich the *Prince of this world*,
ere amongst men; yea how vi-
rè transformed into his image
odigious and desperat acts of
as we should think humane
not but tremble at. IV. That
rol the certainty both of *sense*
ich is in the truth of *apparitions*
ssions of men in all ages, and in
he earth ; and can need no de-
or this, that in many places of
e *devil* is both visibly and audi-
V. That he is so manifest in
e as a *spirit of blasphemy*, which
acts men to war against hea-

ven

ven with their *tongue* in such oathes and cur-
sing as hath no casual pleasure, or gain herein; yea, as a *spirit of delusion* in so visible ane
excitement of others to these extravagancies
under a shew of religion, as are incompatible with any use of judgement or reason.
V I. That so innumerable a company of humane race, hath in all ages been in a *formal*,
and *expresse covenant* with these powers of
darknesse is undenyable upon the most severe and impartial inquiry herein.

Qu. II. What special *assistence* to your
faith doth the certainty of these *powers* of
darknesse bring therewith?

Answ. I. That such a party both in their
nature and continued actings, are in a stated
opposition to the Kingdome of Christ.
I I. That it is so visible the *prey* which these
mighty hunters do follow is not our *body*, or
the things of this life, but is with respect to
ane *immortal soul*, and ane *after state*, and
that thus man might be made sharer of the
same misery under which they are concluded. I I I. That all may see their being under restraint of a supream power above them
& under such *chaines* as do irresistibly bound
their *rage*, and *enmity* against man by ane
invisible guard and *hedge* which they cannot
breake over. I V. How their greatest rage, and strugling is against the *conversion*,
of

of sinners to God, and to hold fast his pos-
session in such, as the *Spirit of God* doth not,
more clearly move for their rescue, then
these doe to crosse that blessed design of the
Gospel. V. That there are none serious
in the truth and life of religion but finde
themselves pursued by such ane *adversary*;
and to have as discernably another party
then themselves, or the world to conflict
with as if they saw them in *a visible shape.*
V I. That by the *Gospel* and within the precinct of the church, is so discernably a greater *restraint of Satans dominion* and power then
in all the earth besides; yea that the advantage of being within the *external covenant of
Baptisme*, is so demonstrable as the least yeel-
ding or tendency to a renouncing of the same, or any acts of *homage*, for making use
of his help, hath ever made way for some
more extraordinary power of the *devil* over
such then others. V I I. Thus also is a most
undeniable confirmation given of ane *invisible world*, and of such *intellectual beings* there, as are far above man; yea that there is
so undoubted ane intercourse betwixt men
and spirits, as may clearly shew that interest
mens soul hath in another state and world
then this.

Qu. I I I. Is that great truth of the *immortality of the soull*, and its never dying sta-

E 3   te

te after death, as fully demonstrable to reason, as it is by the furtheft certainty of
faith?

ANSW. Though it be fo amazing a thing
to beleeve ane *immortal foull*, and *eternal fla-
te*, wherein it muft shortly enter, as by few
feemes to be apprehended, yet are its demonftrative evidences, fuch that except
men lofe all fence and ufe of reafon, it is
not poffible to deny. I. That there is fuch
ane *immaterial and active fubftance* as the
foull, which can admit no caufe, either of
its decay or diffolution, from the body, yea
that the greateft excellency of this vifible
creation, is here, that fuch a vital *beam of*
life, *light*, and *immortality*, as the *foull* of
man is therein. II. Though we cannot fee
this rare and wonderful being, yet it is here
we both *fee*, and *feel* it to be fomething *di-*
ftinct from the body, and to have a diftinct intereft, both in its griefs and comforts.
III. How it can have no dependance on the
body in its being, which doth no way depend thereon in its actings and exercife; but
is oft moft vigorous and cleare, in its exercife, not only when moft *feparat* and abftract
from fenfible things, but when the *flesh* is
under the greateft decay, and neare its *dif-*
fo'ution; to shew the *foull* lyeth not a dying
with the body, but hath its *diftinct fubfiften-*
ce,

ce, to live in a separat ftate, when it dyes.
IV. Its being peculiarly framed for converfe, and intercourfe with fpiritual beings,
yea is only of the vifible creation admit to
fellowship with the invifible God, and to
have reflex acts upon it felf. V. How it is
a *being* of a higher nature and value, then
the fun, moon and ftarrs; which not only
can know, and conceive of things above the
evidence and impreffions of *fenfe*, but to
make a rational choife of good, though croffe to any fenfual pleafure ; yea to rejoyce,
and have its proper delights; when the body is afflicted and in pain ; nor can be defiled
from the moft loathfome fores and defile-
ments of the flesh, fo as I muft needs fee
both its dominion and preheminence over
the body, and to have affuredlie a fubfiftence.
without the fame. VI. That it is fuch a being,
as is capable of a happineffe beyond the whole extent of the world, & hath thefe intellectual facultyes, which cannot poffibly want,
both objects fuitable thereto, and injoyments, above the fenfes. VII. That the
moft choife and excellent, are ufually moft
afflicted, and crushed under the feet of their
oppreffours, whilft thefe flourish in the
earth and have no bands in their death; fo as,
fuch were of all men the moft miferable, if
in this life, both their being and bleffedneffe

E 4   were

were founded. VIII. That there is fo univerfal a fenfe of immortality, as thefe who
both feare and hate the evidences hereof,
yet under fome conftraint of reafon hath the
fame for a continued terrour. IX. That it
is fure the *certainty of death*, makes it fimply impoffible, for things only fuited to
this life of fenfe, to be the ultimate good,
or fruition of man; fince elfe the *beafts*
fhould have a greater happineffe then fuch,
if it were not from refpect to ane after and
immortal ftate.

Qu. IV. What confirmation to your
faith does that great and amazing change by
death offer, when it would feem to be fomething meerly *natural?*

Answ. Though the only wife God
moves herein according to the nature of fecond caufes, and that it hath various wayes
of approach unto men, yet may all fee with
the furtheft conviction of rational evidence,
as well as certainty of faith, I. How *death in
its firft conftitution is penal*; and comes by a
divine appointment unto all, not meerly as
men but as finners, and to be thus no *natural accident* and refult of our primitive and
original frames. II. That its *death*, as a *penalty* which keepes the feare and dread thereof fo much on all living, as th it laft period,
when the eternal ftate of men is then caft.

III,

III. That the *sting* and bitternesse of sin, is
so manifest in innumerable diseases and
stroakes of death, which many feel an 100.
times ere they *dye* once, beyond other of the
creatures. IV. Though the sentence of
dying is on all, yet so great a difference is betwixt the saints and residue of men here, that
its *penal* execution on the ungodly, is such
as nature can give no support herein. V.
That *supernatural presages* and warnings
hereof ere it come, are in all times so known
and sure; yea such extraordinare evidences
sometimes of the precise time, as could have
no possible rise from any *natural cause*. VI.
That its immediat *commission* from a supream
and *invisible power*, is so evident in such exe-
cutions oft, of this sentence, by *sword*,
famine and *pestilence*, as the visible *finger of
God*, in a just retribution unto men for sin,
may be no lesse seen, and a supernatural *cau-
sality*, then the effects have been undoubted
and cleare; to shew such is the state of man,
as this great revolution by *death*, doth each
moment depend on a call from heaven.
VII. That the certainty of something *supernatural* herein, as the King of terrours, is
so, known as no releefe can possibly be
found, but in the *truth and power of Christianity*, to set men both above the feare of
death and ane after state, when once it comes

E 5 . neere.

neere. VIII. Yea that it is furely above the
poffibility of nature, which can beare out in
this great adventure and *trial* of mens *faith*,
both in the truth and ftrength thereof, at
death, for which end the Lord hath thus,
choifed that by fo ftrange ane *entry*, and at
fo dark a port they fhould firft paffe to the
full enjoyment of that glorious ftate a-
bove.

Qu. V. What *evidence* and *demonftration* can yow fhew, to confirm fo great a
faith of an *eternal glory* abiding the Saints
in heaven, and of its *earneft* and *firft fruits*
here, as may ftrike ane undeniable conviction hereof on the world?

Answ. I. By that vifible *ripening* and refemblance to fuch a ftate in all the degrees of
a Chriftians grouth, to a more *full ftature of
the man in Chrift*, as may be no leffe evident
then the natural grouth of our body. II.
That though the opening of thefe *gates* of
the *fecond world* be hid, as no humane fenfe
can difcern the *fpirit* in its *afcent* through
thefe higher regions, to that unconceiveable *paradife and glory* in the *third heaven*, yet
is the *triumphant entry* and paffage of innumerable Chriftians at death, fuch as hath
oft been, a matter of fenfe and cleareft evidence to the world. III. That fuch alfo
were both *humble*, *tender*, and *fincere* in
their

their life, and then in so great a composure of judgement, as all might see they knew what made them glade and could swallow up both the feares and bitternesse of death; yea that this was not given for their own support only, but for a more *publick use*, to the conviction and confirming of others. IV. That the state of glory is demonstrable and hath been oft brought downe to mens sense, by these *ravishing joyes of the Martyres of Christ*, and exultation of spirit even in the *flames*. V. By such supernaturall comforts as attend the life of Christianity, and can have no possible rise from the flesh and outward causes, with that *joy and peace*, which by so natural a result followes *welldoing*; and any service of love for Christ as all may see to be the *first fruits* of that harvest which is above. VI. By so rare and marvellous a frame of the *new man*, set up in this lower region of grace, in so discernable a conformity to the blessed God, and resemblence to another state then here, to which the world is but as a place of pilgrimage, trial and a *preparatory state*. only. VII. By such visible returns of joy and comfort of Christians after saddest conflicts and downecastings, and day-break of these *vital quickning beames of divine light*, that have been no lesse evident oft, then that of

the

the *martyrs* at the ftake , who cryed out ;
Now he is come, he is come. V.I I I. By thefe
breathings of love after ane unfeen Chrift
and vifible effects of its power on men, as
might shew fome begun *tranflation* of the
foull fo far herein, as to be more where it
loves then it lives. I X. Though we cannot fee here, that *ineffable glory*, which is
above, but should have our *faith* infteed of
eyes; yet fuch is the truth of *holineffe* , as
doth not only evi.'ence, but in its own nature partake of a *future glory*; fo as every
degree and act thereof doth enter in a begun ftate of *fruition* and blessedneffe , and
makes it fimply impoffible for a *good man* in
any true exercife of godlinefs, *not to be hap-*
py alfo, and thus in a more near capacity to
know that *joy unfpeakable*, and *full of glory*,
which is above. X. By fo fure, known,
and tryed a paffage betwixt heaven and mens
fouls in *prayer*, with fo fetled a trade of *com-*
merce this way, and certain returns, as with
affurance fuch can fay, though they muft
change *their place* , yet not their *company*.
X'. That the whole difpenfations of providence in *Ifraels paffage* through the *wilder-*
neffe, and to fo excellent a country as *Ca-*
naan, is no leffe fure in it felf, then that i
was given for an embleme and *type* of the jurt
nying and militant ftate of the faints here :
and,

and to be a solemne pledge of that *Canaan a-
bove.* XII. That such is the magnificence,
harmony, and order of these visible *heavens,*
and *celestial bodies* there, with their different
degrees of *glory*, (though all illuminated from
the same fountain of light the sun) as we
may judge by a *divine ordination* have some
peculiar respect to that end, to awake & raise
our thoughts thus, to these *higher regions of
glory*, which are above all these; by what is
thus visible to our eyes; where the redeemed
of the Lord shall be ever fixed , & *shine forth
as the Sun in the kingdome of their Father.*

Qu. VI. What visible and awakning
evidences are there of the truth of an *Hell*,
and that state of *horrour* and *torment* in another world, which even to mens *senses* here,
might present the certainty thereof?

Answ. I. That it can be no more sure,
there is such a power and party as that of the
Devils, then the reality of some such *horrid
region* and place also, to which they belong,
and are adjudged to. II. From so innumerable a company of *human race*, as are not
only in the visible service of these *infernal
spirits*, but partakers of the same nature and
enmity against the *H. God* and his *image*, as
doth clearly witnesse their respect and tendency to the same *state* and *place*, and to be
confederate in their *judgement*, as they were
here

here in their *sin*. III. From such visible impressions of *vindictive justice* on mens souls, with such *horrour of conscience* and unsufferable torments this way, as in all ages have been known by most remarkable instances, when not in the least distemper of their natural reason, that may present to mens *senses* something of a *visible Hell*, as convincingly, as if one had *risen from the dead*, for the same. IV. From such a trembling *sense*, and *terror of divine vengeance*, as oft follows upon *horrid acts of wickednesse* and most eminently then breaks forth upon a surprising sight of *death*; as all may see something more dreadful herein then the dissolution of nature and the power and present arrest of a *future judgment* made visible in the same. V. From such begun degrees, as that of *blaspheming and rage* against God; because of his *plagues*, with these *prodigies of cruelty* exerced by men here in the earth; as might be evident to all to be more then human, and rather the effects of infernal spirits acting in a human shape: VI. From so clear a *prelude* of the same in that judicial *obduration*, and blindnesse, so many are given up to under the greatest discoveries of light, so as all may see their being thus bound over in *chains*, and shut up in *prison*, until *death* bring them forth to the

exe-

execution; and how no relief or application of the means of grace hath then any more accesse. VII. From such a mape & shaddow of *eternal vengeance*, in these terrible acts of divine judgment inflicted here on *Apostates*, and *persecuters* of the *truth*, and other flagitious persons which with the very first view might present an awful and immediat appearence of God in the same, and that some *strang* and supernatural *punishment* is oft visible on the *workers of iniquity*. VIII. And what ever be of natural causes in such visible represfentations here in the earth, as that *sulphureous lake* where once *Sodom* was, and these burning mountains such as *Hæcla*, *Etna*, and *Vesuvius*, yet we may truely judge their being thus set before the world as some visible memorials of these *infernal flames*; and as it were so many *lumeheads* thereof, for such who will not believe the same, because they doe not yet see or feal such a thing.

Qu. VII. What *assistances* hath our *faith*, of that great and wonderful truth of the *resurrection of the body*, after its dissolution in the *grave unto dust*?

Answ. I. From that visible and stupendious frame of the *heavens* and the *earth*, when its sure that the same *infinite power*, that hath not only made man, but the whole creation, can as easily collect and recount the

the difperfed *ashes* of the *body*, as *form the same.* II. From that greateft pledge hereof, in the *refurrection of the body of Chrift.* III. From that tribulation and fore pain, that the faints here in their outward man are ex-pofed to, fince it is fure that in the holy juftice of God, he did not give fuch *bodies* for *labour*, and for toyl; and to his *martyrs*, to endure unexpreffible torments for Chrift, to perifh for ever. IV. From thefe vifible *refemblances* and *prefigurations* of the *refurrection* which the Lord hath given to confirme our faith herein, in the ordinare courfe and *productions of nature*; fo as all may fee how every *night* is as the *grave* of the *daylight*, and each morning a new refurrection of the fame; and how vifible an image of *death* is in each feafon of the *winter*, with fo marvelous and beatiful a *refurrection* of the earth, on every return of the fpring, in the *herbs, flowers and plants*, taking life and ri-fing again, in the *leaves, bloffomes and fruites*; yea this in fuch a variety, as may no leffe convincingly evidence an infinite divine power herein, then that the fame body of man fhould be raifed at the *laft day.* V. From that continued *miracle* of the *harveft*, after the *feed-time*, with fo amazing a pro-duction of the *grain fowen* in the earth, and its firft dying there before it be quickned,

fo

so as to be at last brought to 30, 60, yea sometimes an *hundred fold*, out of the very same grain; which to these who had never before known the same would seem incredible, & above all reason to conceave, or bear credite therto.

CHAPTER III.

The confirming worke of Religion, *impro-ven wich respect to the* times, *to* clear the way of the Lord *herein*, *before this gene-ration*, *and let us see how nothing is so strang in the* events *of this day*, *which should not more strenthen, then shake, and that the* God of the Reformed Church *doth still own the same interest*, *according to his* faithful-nesse: *which is here briefly pointed at*, *upon some special* inquiry, *proposed about the same.*

SECTION I.

Qu. WHat can afford both *light*, and *confirmation to our faith*, in such a time, when we see the *worke of the Lord*, about his Church, to be most remarkably now a *worke of judgement*, with such dark and searching tryals therwith, as former times have not known.

F   ANSW.

Answ. It is fure, we have feen nothing; but what might have been too evidently looked for, and that we can pretend no want of *light* herein, upon thefe grounds. I. That the *Trialls* of a Church, should be fuited to the meafure of their *talent of light*, & when this hath been in fome more then ordinare way difpenfed, that fome remarkably *fearching times* might be expected to follow; nor can it be now ftrang to us, that fuch things fall in with this *day*, which did not meet the *Churches* of *Chrift* at the *firft entry of the Reformation*, who then had not fo clear difcoveries of the truth, and that meafure of *confirmation* therein, which hath been fince. II. That fome unufual *tryals*, and *conflicts*, in the Lords ufuall method of providence, should be fuited alfo, to the greatneffe of that *worke*, which he is bringing forth, may be no ftrang thing; and to fee a time of fuch fore wreftlings as this, when all things feem to cry, *be in pain* as *Micah* 4: 20. Yea when fome great *event* of the Scripture is to be revealed to the world, and near to its *full hight*, and *period of accomplifhment*, as we have fafe ground for affurance of this day. III. Nor hath this fad and difmal hower on the Church, been more obvious then the *provoking caufe* hereof, in which the *holy righteoufneffe of God*, may be

no

no leffe clear then the *cloud* now is dark; when fuch a vifible falling of hath been from that *love* , *tendernes* , and *power of religion* that did formerly attend its profeffion; as for thefe many years paft we might have feen that fome fore and remarkable judgment was coming, and that if we had not been in fuch a maner undone , we were , under fome fadder ftrock of fpiritual judgment, ready to be undone. IV. Yea it hath been too vifible, that fuch *evils* followed the *Reformed Churches* , as in no time it was ever known, that the holy God, did paffe fuch by, without fome fignal evidence of his *wrath* againft the fame before the world. V. We know that *carnal confidence* hath a *curfe* ever waiting upon it in the *Scripture*, which none can take of, or make that thrive which God hath himfelf curfed; and it is too vifible how far we have gone thus out of the way of our ftrenth , by fuch eager feeking *human props* , & fupport, as we have forgot the *guide of our youth* , and *convenant of our God* , and what great things he hath formerly done in the greateft ftraits of his Church, when there was much humble *trufting* , with little fence; as though the *fpirit of the Lord* , had not done more to recover his truth; then all human might or power, ever could doe.

SEC-

SECTION II.

Qu. WHat talent, are we ftill accountable for to fupport our faith,
againft the greateft *fears* of this time, from
thefe *immediate appearences of God*, and of the
glory of his power, for the fame *truth and caufe* of the *Reformed Church*, we are now called to contend for, which hath been fince
the reformation when fo ftrong & unufual a
tyde, now is againft the fame?

ANsw. If men fhut not their eyes, and
hide this great *talent* of the *workes of God*, *under the ground*, its fure none can queftion
fuch a *feal*, which before the fun, to the a-
mazment and conviction of the world, hath
been put to the truth of the *Reformed Religion*; that we are now fifted under fuch a *call*,
as the Church of *Ifrael* was, *Deut.* 4: 34.
to *ask of the times, that are paft*, fince *Ifraels* coming out of Egypt, and fince the
firft planting of the *Gentil Church*, by the
Gofpel, *whither there hath been fo great a thing
as this in the earth*, *that God hath effayed to take to himfelf a people from the midft of other nations*, by *temptations*, *by figns*, *and by wonders*, and *by war*, and by *a mighty hand*, and
by *an ouftretched arm*, and *by great terrours*,
according to all that the *Lord our God* hath
done

done for the refcue of his people, in thefe *laft times*, from *Antichriftian* bondage and darkneffe; and fettling them in a church ftate; but *unto us was this shewed , that we might know, that the Lord he is God, and there is none elfe befide him :* yea are ftill called to fee, and be as *eye witneffes* to thefe things; I. How *bright a day* of the Gofpel of Chrift, did goe before this great *darkneffe* on the Church , and what a folemne *triumph* in thefe late ages the *truth* hath had over *Antichrift*; fo as the *full ftrock* and ruine of his kingdome, which is fure and eftablished in the *promife of God*, feems not now more marvelous and above human appearence, then what *we have feen*, in the begun degrees of its accomplishment. I I. In how few years alfo , there was, as a *new Chriftian world* brought forth , in that fwift courfe and progreffe which the ingathering of the Reformed Churches had ; fo as between the year 1621, and 1560. fuch famous *plantations* of the Gofpel, were fetled in a Church ftate; which all may fee was the immediate worke and power of God ; to shew that none should fear, or *ftagger at his promife*, though the waters yet fwell, and come to the *flowings of Jordan*; and difficulties appear unfuperable to human fenfe, after this great things which the Lord hath done. I I I. How extraordinare a *calling*, and

ex-

excitment of *instruments*, was then evident,
for the service of that time, and *reapers* thus
eminently prepared for so great an *harvest* of
the Gospel, as might put the world to inquire whence these were, in so numerous a concurrence, when a few of such a spirit, were so rarely to be found in many ages before.
IV. Yea such an accession also, of *spiritual*
gifts, and induments then for *building* of the
Church, as had not been formerly known,
since the first coming of the Gospel to the
Gentils; wherein it may be said, the *glo-*
ry of these *last times* hath even in some degree
exceeded that of the *first*. V. And can the
most dismal things of this time, countervail
the *confirmations of our faith*, who have so
clearly seen, with the first breaking up of
the *pur doctrine of Christ*, the *power and life*
of Christianity came therwith to the world,
as a *seal*, and attestation therto, beyond
any *miracles*; yea how innumerable a company, in these last ages of different tongues
and languages, and these so remot from one
another, did not only receive the same truth,
but with such resolution adventure their
souls theron, as might fully witnesse, they
had another prospect of *Christianity*, and to
be in some other manner ravished with the
glory & *beuty* of the same; then is now in
these times. VI. That such high *spring ty-*

des of the *power*, and *efficacy* of the Gospel, might be evident to all, after so sad a restraint had been for so many ages before, under *Antichristian* darknesse; for whatever was then as a *private seall*, on the spirit of Christians whilst the witnesses did *prophesy in sack-cloth*, yet was there no such evidence and *demonstration of the H. Ghost*, or a *publick confirmatory seal* to the truth, as was after the *Reformation*. ·VII. Yea was it not the most sober, serious, and inquisitive part of men, upon a sure tryal of the grounds of their faith, who did most firmly imbrace the same; and how many of these also were of the greatest parts and abilities, whom none could judge to adventure so far herein, without the highest assurances, that this was their undoubted interest and upmaking. VIII. We have seen not only these of mean and low estate, but such of the *highest* place and *quality*, most chearfully adventuring whatever interest could be dearest to them, in the earth for the truths sake; yea was ever found, how such as were most acquaint, with the reformed religion in its power, and living up in their practise, to what they profest thereof, were these who with the greatest assurance, have most resoluty still adhered thereto. IX. We have seen also, its most remarkable spreading in the world,

when

when there could be no poſſible pretence of
a *lucrative intereſt*, or external motives for
the ſame.　X. We have ſeen ſomething not
only extraordinare, but even *miraculous* in
the *joy*, and *reſolution* of innumberable *mar-*
tyrs ſince the *Reformation* who did bear out
with a more then human ſtrenth, againſt a
cruelty ſo viſibly *inhuman*, and ſavage; yea
which did in ſome degrees exceed that meaſure of the *Heathens*, in the *Primitive times*,
as being againſt a greater light then theirs.
I I. And have we not ſeen of what ſpirit,
ſuch ſtill have been ſince the *Reformation*,
who were the moſt notour inſtruments in
the Churches perſecution; and how viſibly
ſuch did act herein, under ſo impetuous an
incitment of the *Devil*, that as *Tertullien*, in
his *Apollogy* ſpeaks of *Nero*, the truth might
boaſt in having ſuch adverſaries.　X I I. It
is ſure we have ſeen, how no human power,
could yet ever undoe this bleſſed intereſt of
the *Reformed religion*, tho no way, or change of weapons, hath been left untryed; but
we have thus ſeen, whither ſo ſtrong, and
unite a confederacy, as the *Catholick league*
in *France* did at laſt reſolve, and, not only
in the ruine of the greateſt acters and contri-
vers therein, but to a further eſtabliſhing of
the *Reformed Church* there, as though ſuch
had intentionally acted for the ſame; when

if

if *second causes* had brought forth their ordinare effects, it might have been judged impoſſible to fail. XIII. We have ſeen that
iſſue of the whole councels, expenſe and
cruelty of *Philip the II. of Spain*, to bear
down the truth of the Goſpel in the *Nether-
lands*, which was to the furtheſt ſetling of
this *illuſtrious ſtate* and the *Church of Chriſt*
there; yea how their conſpicuous riſe and
flowriſhing even in the externals, and their
reſolute adherence to the truth of Chriſt did
moſt viſibly keep together. XIV. We
know that *deludge of blood*, which ſo quickly followed the *French maſſacre*; and the
moſt diſmal time which ever that *nation*
know, did then viſibly contemporate, with
ſuch a time of their greateſt rage and perſecution againſt the truth, and that event of
the *third vial* moſt clearly fulfilled herein,
Revel. 16: 5,6. *Thou art righteous, ó Lord,
which art, and was, and ſhall be, becauſe
thou haſt judged thus, for they have ſhed the
blood of thy ſaints and prophets, and thou haſt
given them blood to drink in great meaſure.*
XV. Yea have we not ſeen how *four Kings
of France* ſucceſſively were in leſſe then 30.
years, taken away; in the ſame continued
purſuit, how to deſtroy the Church there,
in whom that whole race of the *Valois* was
thus extinct; yea in the manner of their

death,

death, were moft remarkable monuments of divine judgement, as the moft famous writers of that time does atteft. XVI. We have feen what marvelous effects did follow thefe bloody years of *Queen Mary's reign* in England, to promot and commend the Proteftant doctrine to mens confciences there, with fo great a triumph it had in the fufferings of fuch choife and excellent witneffes for Chrift, as hath brought in more rent to the praife and glory of their bleffed head, then may to the furtheft compenfe all that blood of the Saints there, though highly *precious in the eyes of the Lord.* XVII. We have feen likewayes the blood and cruelty, of late againft the Proteftants *in Bohemia*, in a fhort time moft obfervably returned on the authors thereof, and how the immediate finger of God might be feen in calling forth the *Swedes* to avenge the fame, and in that defolating ftrock which followed on *Germany.* XVIII. We have feen in thefe late times the iffue of that horrid *maffacre* on the *Proteftants in Ireland*, to the utter ruine in a very few years after, of that barbarous party, who had thus acted herein. XIX. We have feen what wonderful providences did attend the actings of that poor handful of *Proteftants* in the *Valleys of Piemont* fince the *Reformation*, upon the account of that
bloody

bloody *maffacre* which was fet on foot there
againft them , which was fo aftonishing as
all might fee an extraordinare appearence of
the Lord herein , as is clearly attefted by
the moft faithful Hiftories of that time.
XX. And can it be forgot unto this day,
how vifibly a divine hand did appear in breaking that great *Spanish Armado*, in the year
1588. which had been for fome years in con-
triving againft *England*. XXI. As it was
aftonishing , and fpecially demonftrative
of the immediate power and prefence of
God , it should be matter of wonder and
praife alfo for after ages, that folemne time
of the *Reformation* of the *Church in Scotland*,
for planting the *reformed Religion* there; with
that zeal and onneffe of fpirit , as did then
appear in all ranks to imbrace and adhere to
the profeffion thereof, amidft the greateft
threatnings of their adverfaries; fo as a *few
years* did bring forth that, which would have
feemed ftrang for an *age* to accomplish ; yea
that we find betwixt the laft *Martyr* for the
truth there, who was *burnt at St. Andrews*
1558. and the eftablishment of the *Proteftant
Religion* , and full abolishment of *Popery*,
with the full concurrence of *civil authority*
herein , in *July* 1560. was but little above
two years ; to shew what great things the
Lord can doe, above all human councel or

con-

confidence. XXII. Its fure we have feen
in what remarkable degrees thefe *loft vials*
of the holy judgment of God, hath taken
place on the Kingdome of *Antichrift*, and
how confpicuous the *event* hath been of that
prophecy, 2 *Theffal.* 2: 8. in thefe great effects and confumption thereof by the miniftry of the Gofpel, as an affured pledge of
the full accomplifhment of what remains
herein. XXIII. And as every ftep of the
Churches rife, hath been ftill advanced in a
continued conflict betwixt the *truth and
Antichrift*, fo have we ftill feen, when the
affault and oppofition hath been greateft, its
moft remarkable tendancy to a greater victory; which were it rightly confidered upon
clear and folid grounds from the Scripture,
the moft formidable appearences of trouble from this adverfary fhould with more
comfort then fear this day be looked on; fo
that whatever be the neareft and moft immediate events, yet is it fure, as *the Lord is
true*, whofe word is paffed hereon, that
whofoever gives their power and ftrength
to fupport that intereft of *Antichrift* fhall
lofe the day and find their caufe defperate,
for the party with whom they contend herein is the Son of God, againft whom no human power fhall ever be able to ftand.
Thefe are but a *few*, which are here mentioned,

tioned, of the great *acts of our God*; in behalf of his Truth, to be ſtill as preſent in our ſight, in a time when the ſpirits of many are ready to ſtagger and faint; and here mentioned, to lay no ſtreſſe or weight of the *authority* of the truth and doctrine of our profeſſion thereon, but on the alone *revelation of the Scripture*; but that they are ſuch an undenyable ſeal for confirming our faith, and of ſo known, *publick* and *famous evidence*, as ſhould be no leſſe conſidered and taken to heart now, then in the time when the Lord thus appeared herein.

SECTION III.

Qu. WHat *preſent judgment* are we called to have of this *time*, upon clear and aſſured grounds from the *Scripture*; that we may know under what *aſpect* therof, the preſent *ſtate of Religion* and of the *reformed Churches* is under, when ſo great a *criſis* is this day, as would ſeem to be in the very ἀκμη of its conflict, whither as to life or death?

Answ. It is no preſent appeerances of the time muſt direct our faith, nor ſhould we either ſtreath our fears or expectations of things and *events*, beyond what the God of truth doth warrand in his word, but its
clear,

clear, if we credite the fame, and admitt
the *divinity of the New Teſtament*, there is
no juſt cauſe of heſitation or darkneſſe as to
what the Lord is bringing forth for his
Church now in theſe latter dayes; nor can
there be any pretence, to ſeek an other
light; either from the *ſtars* above, or the
diviners of this time, when ſo woful a trade
hath got up in the world, that men will thus
goe *to the God of Ekron*, as though there were
not *a God in Iſrael*, or ſuch a thing, as his
written Oracles to inquire at, when its ſure
theſe ly open, and with a clear and diſtinct
ſound ſpeaks to all who have a ſerious and
unprejudged ſpirit. I. That the *Church* under the *New Teſtament* hath now paſſed and
gone through that moſt diſmal and continued *tryal* herein, which was to goe over
her head under *Antichriſts reigne* and *hight*;
and whatever appearence he now hath in
great wrath, yet is it ſure and evident that
the *winter is paſt* and the *Churches ſpring* begun; and a few ſteps further of that judgment which is now haſtning on, will at lenth
end the quarrel; ſo that by a near converſe
with the word, we may clearly ſee from what
point the *Churches courſe* and motion this day
lyes, and how exactly it keeps, in the certainty thereof, by that clear *conduct* of the *Scriptures of truth*, where a full *map* of her whole
courſe

tourfe and paffage through time is clearly shewed. II. That we may now with fome clear evidence judge, and have our faith perfwaded hereof, that the *Churches* intereft is upon the *rifing hand*, and on a prefent advance, though nothing would feem more contradictory then all vifible grounds now are; fince this cannot fail, *John.* 3: 30. that *Jefus Chrift* in his kingdom in the earth *muft increafe*; yea that the Scripture fo clearly points forth *Antichrifts* ruine and progreffe of his fall and douncafting, with refemblance to that great judgment on *Pharaoh* as an evident *type* hereof; in the fame judicial ftrocks of *induration*, on both, and *gradual* progreffe herein by one *plague* after another, until the laft and greateft affault, as was then at the *Red-fea*, hath the fame effect for a more glorious appearence of God, in the greateft ftep of judgment, and victory over this adverfary, when not only the *fong of Mofes* but of the *Lamb* alfo fhall be then *fung*, *Rev.* 15: 3. as importing fomething more glorious and a greater brightneffe to be put on this *illuftrious act of divine judgment*, referved to thefe laft times, when a more *immediate appearence of the Lord* will be feen, then in any former deliveries of his Church. III. It is no conjectural thing, but what by a clear Scripture conduct we may fee, that this

time

time of the *Church* now under fo notable a
Crifis in her cafe , is evidently falling under
that *remarkable affault and conflict*, with that
adverfary , before the accomplishing of
that *vial* on *his feat and throne* , as we may
fee *Revel.* 17: 13,14. that when fo confpicuous a ftep of the *Churches victory* is near ;
the oppofition thereto alfo will be in fome
higher degree proportionable to the fame,
when the great men of the earth , and fuch
who shall receive power as Kings , *one hower*
with the beaft , shall have one mind and give
their power and ftrength thereto , and *shall make*
war with the Lamb , *but the Lamb shall over-*
come them , *for he is King of Kings and Lord of*
Lords , &c. Nor is it found through the
Scripture where any *great thing* , the Lord
hath done for his Church , but fome unufual *darkneffe* , and *fore wreftlings* hath ftill
gone before , and should be no matter of
ftaggering to our faith , whatever be of prefent fears , to fee fo difmal a *time of tryal* as
now is, and amazing hight of trouble beyond
what former times have known , when one
of the *greateft events* of providence in behalf
of the Church , fince the revealing of *Chrift*
to the world , until his *fecond coming* , is affuredly near in the fall and overthrow of the
man of fin. I V. We have clear ground
alfo to judge , that fo great an *eclipfe* as feems
allmoft

allmoſt univerſally over the ſtate of the Reformed *Churches*, is no goeing *down of the*
ſun theron, whatever did befall the moſt
famous *eaſtern Churches* to an utter diſſipa-
tion thereof; if theſe different *periodes* of
time be juſtly conſidered, how their *ſun-ſet*
did then fall in with the *entry* of that *great*
Apoſtacy of the Chriſtian Church and with
that long and diſmall night of *Antichriſts*
reign; whilſt now this hower of tryal on the
Churches, doth meet in that bleſſed *period*
of Antichriſts begun fall, and of a growing
light of the Goſpel, and when the *Scripture*
ſo clearly warrands our faith herein, that the
worke of providence is to *plant*, and not *cutt*
of, but to bring forward that intereſt of the
Reformed Churches, in the founding of which
the *Mediator* hath ſo eminently appeared in
the glory of his power in theſe *laſt times*.
V. It is ſure me now live in the evening, and
extremity of time, when the motions of
providence may be expected to be more
quick and ſpeady, as being ſo near the center, and to the laſt *Epocha*, and period of all
prophetick Chronology; wherein the glory of
God in his truth and faithfulneſſe ſhall moſt
eminently ſhine forth, and theſe Scripture
truths which were formerly dark & abſtruſe,
with that evidence ſhine forth in the event,
as ſhall cauſe men to wonder at their former

G   thoughts

thoughts and ftumblings thereat. And here I muft fay, that there is fuch a fight now in the earth, as the *Romifh Church*, in its complex frame and ftate, in fo different a mould caft from any power or jurifdiction elfe, and fuch a compound of a *civil, and Spiritual Monarchy* in one and the fame perfon, is fo folemn and undenyable a *feal* to the *Chriftian faith*, and *divinity of the New Teftament*; that its ftrang why this is not improven more, againft the *Atheifm* of this time, that fuch a vifible event of the Scripture is now in being, which was fo clearly fortold by the *Holy Ghoft* 1500. years ago, with its proper circumftances, as to the manner of that *Antichriftian ftate*, with its *rife, growth, & duration*, as is to admiration ftil evident to the world, when not the leaft shaddow or appearence of fo ftrang future emergencies was to be feen or could have entred in mens thoughts; to shew it only could be revealed to the Church by him, to whom all his works are known from the beginning. This I have looked on, as fuch a *confirmation* to the truth of Chriftianity, that no miracles in the firft times of the Church could have more evidence for the fame; yea if fuch a party were not in being, both what it now is and in former ages hath been, it might in another manner ftagger the faith of the

Saints,

Saints, to a queſtioning the truth of the Scripture, then its moſt formidable appearence this day can doe. VI. I ſhall but add here, that we know and are ſure the Lord hath reſerved his greateſt works to theſe latter dayes, wherein his judgments ſhall be manifeſt; and that one of the moſt eminent manifeſtations of his glory before the cloſe of time ſhal be conſpicuous in the *fall of Antichriſt*, on whoſe ruines that *glorious hous* which Chriſt is yet to have for himſelf both of *Jews* and *Gentiles*, ſhall be prepared and built up ; and though this great *eclipſe* of *Antichriſtian darkneſſe*, ſhould yet more prevail, even over the viſible profeſſion of the truth in the *Churches* of *Britain*, and *Ireland*, there is no cauſe to be ſtaggered in the faith of *Romes fatal period*, being near, but to look hereon according to the Scripture as the *Ultimus Conatus* of that wounded adverſary, which will be found in the iſſue to have the moſt immediate connexion with his greateſt downfall, and the *reviving glory* of the *Church* ; for *ſtrong is the Lord God who judgeth her.*

SECTION IV.

Qu. WHat is *ſpecially called for*, in this day, of ſuch as are accoun-

table

table for fo great a talent of light, and confirmations to our faith?

_A n s w._ If this were fuitably taken to heart, we could not but reckon our felves under the greateft excitment and _call_, to fuch an improvment hereof.

I. That we account it not enough to have a _faith_, for quieting our own fpirits, but how to _confirme_ others, by _putting to our feal that God is true_, in the great affurances of his word, and to _fanctify him before the world_, which is fo important a duty, as the Lord was wroth even with a _Mofes_, and _Aaron_ for one short-coming, when he called for the fame, _Numb._ 20: 12. and its fure in no time was fuch a fpecial truft more repofed thereon, then in this age, both as a publick debt on the Church, & perfonal on each Chriftian, how to witneffe for the Lord, upon that great intereft of his faithfulneffe and for tranfmitting the fame, to the ages to come, by a confirmatory feal, and teftimony therto.

II. To reckon our felves alfo under fome more then ordinare _call_ this day, each in their prefent capacity and ftation, how to appear for the _credite_ of the truth, and _ftemm_ fo vifible and impetuous a _tyde_, as is now running of _diftruct_, and of a difcreditable _faint_; for it may be faid, never was the _Church_ under

der

der the *New Testament* so remarkably sisted
under such a trial, as that wherein the Lord
did *prove* the *Church of Israel, Numb.* 14. or
had a more evident resemblance therto, in
the same circumstances as in this day, if they
were seriously pondered ; as I how in the same manner , such a false & *evil report* is too
visibly raised upon the blest ways of the
Lord , to discourage and faint the spirits of
his people, as was then by the *spyes* , that
there were insuperable difficulties in the way
of the promise , by reason of the *Anakims*,
and of their *walled cities*, and did thus op-
pose the credite of *sense*, to all these *assurances which God had given to their faith.* II. That
this highly dishonourable faint and *distrust*
did so sease on that people, as was like to
resolve in a visible revolt , and to *cry for a lea-
der* to *goe back to Egypt* again ; which amongst
too many in this time may be justly feared.
III. That this was after such extraordinare
confirmations which the Lord had given to
the faith of his *Church* then, who had by his
own immediate and outstretched hand so
latly brought them out of the *house of bondage*, and from *the iron furnace in Egypt* , as rendred their misbeliefe to be a guilt under such
aggravations , as the holy God did in that
manner plead, *vers.* 22. *These ten times have
they tempted me, who have seen my glory, and*

G 3   *my*

my miracles, which I did in the wildernesse,
&c. I V. But herein we hope, and are con-
fidently sure of a blessed *disparity* in this resemblance, as to the *numberousnesse* of such,
who shall be found of the *Reformed Churches,*
to act something of that part, which these
heroick witnesses a *Caleb* & *Joshua* did & were
then put to stand alone therein, who through
grat shall yet appear with some measure of
that spirit, and withstand so high a tyde of
fears, discouragment and misbeliefe as is
this day, and thus to plead against the same
as these did, *Num.* 14: 9. if the Lord delight
in us, then let us not rebel against him, neither fear the greatest difficulties can be in the
way &c. V. And is not the same precedent of
providence, of so singular a respect as the Lord
did then testify to his *Caleb* and *Joshua* (who
were of *another spirit* in *following him fully,*
in that day) a continued assurance, for all who
shall be helped to any honourable appearence
of this kind, by making them see, and inherit
the truth of his promise; yea that such a residue who outlives this great and amazing
storme shal have something of that testimony
to bear also which *Caleb* gave *Josh.* 14: 8, 10.
My brethren which went up with me made the
heart of the people faint, but I fully followed
the Lord my God, and now behold the Lord
hath keeped me alive, &c. o blessed they whose
souls

ed, with that holy zeal for the
d up in this great breach, by a
ession of their faith, and wit-
faithfulnesse of God, as such
raordinar confirmations, given
w calls for.

one of the special duties of this
also accomptable for, how to
nigh and growing *tyde of preju-*
roach against the *Reformed Reli-*
n some unusual way is now aloft;
nifestation of the truth to gain
wfull regard herof on mens con-
it they may see somthing of the
profession, and in what maner it
conquest as no way else can pos-

I. Which reckons none else to
and genuine professours hereof,
e not the same upon *evidence,*
pect to its *intrinsick excellency* and
does judge the interest of reli-
e by *number, and poll,* where
ing; but to pursue that end to
gadged *first to be Christians,* that
true and sincere *Protestants;* and
admitt no such methods of any
ance with the humour and in-
en, which its principles will not

Which in its course is ever
certain, according to that rule

G 4   of

of an *uncheangable and eternal truth*, without
dependance on the will of man herein, or
any mutable revolutions of the time. III.
Which doth with the greateft luftre shine
forth in the brighteft *light*, and is maintained
by the *cleareft knowledge*; yea by the furtheft
plaineffe, and openneffe of heart, towards
all, commends it felf; fo that the world may
fee, it efpoufeth not mens *affection*, before
it gain on their *confcience*; and to have their
judgment fixed on a judicious tryal, before
their refolution; nor accounts the truth
of religion, can ever fubfift by an *external
shew* and profeffion, without is known
evidence and the *efficacy* therof on mens foul.
IV. Which fincerly follows the *Catholick
intereft of Chriftianitie* and publick good of
mankind, in promotting the great *ends of the
Gofpel*, fo as the world may fee its higheft intent is to exalt all *divine inftitutions*, and advance the *fimplicity*, and fpirituality of
Gofpel adminiftrations, (according to the
revealed *rule*) amonghft men, as that which
doth moft nearly conceirn the *vitals of religion* and ane *inward life* of communion with
God. V. Which pleads an impartial tryal
of al its adverfaries, whither the principles
of our *profeffion* or of *Popery*, gives the greateft fecurity to *Civil Government*, & founds
the ftrongeft obligations to *Magiftracy* and
to

to all *Civil*, and *Moral duties*, by which
the awe and venerable efteem of religion is
kept up in a nation. It is high time that men
should ceafe to be implicit upon this greateft
intereft they have within time, which is the
truth of their profeffion in the matter of religion, when a deceit or miftake here is of
an eternal conceirn : upon which account
without refpect to intereft, party, or education, I have this day fought to know the
truth, and what adverfaries could poffibly
pretend, to *reproach*, or prejudge any
at the *Reformed Religion*, which can only
amount, to charge mens corruption and of-
fences in their practife, upon the *rule* and
principles of their *profeffion*, that can never
give the leaft *latitude*, or connivance therto,
but is *clear as the fun*; when on the other
hand I could know no other way, to imbrace fuch a profeffion, as *Popery*, but by
turning *Atheift*, in the *firft place*, and quite
both *religion* and *reafon* at once : but may fay,
in a refolute adherence to the doctrine of the
Reformed Church, I fear not to adventure my
foul, and enter in to an eternal ftate.

The

The CONTENTS.

CHAPTER I.

The primitive confirmation, held forth and cleared in seven Positions.

POSIT. I. That sad aspect, which the implicit and traditional profession of this day hath upon the present state of religion.   Pag. 1

POSIT. II. The greatnesse of that service for the Church to have a clear founding of the faith of assent, upon known and solid grounds herein, more universally promott.   3

POSIT. III. The true primitive confirmation as it was in the times of the Apostles, hold forth and cleared from the Scripture.   6

POSIT. IV. The continued necessity therof, no lesse convincing now, for the Churches use, then in these Primitive times.   9

POSIT. V. That such a confirmatory worke respects not only the more knowing and inquisitive part of men, but the meanest within the Church.   11

POSIT. VI. VVhat is specially called for in the practicall use of this primitive confirmation, held forth in some serious proposals for this end.   14

POSIT. VII. VVhat special excitment we are under, for promoting the same in so remarkable a period of time as this, and from that hope of a greater reviving yet of such a Catholick spirit, to advance the highest ends of religion amonghst men.   19

CHAPTER II.

For giving some clear view, of these primary evidences and demonstrations of our faith, that the meanest Christian should know, and vvith the least expense of time may improve for their dayly use, on these greatest principles.

SECTION I.

I. Of the glorious being of God, which is the first foundation of all religion.   22

II. Of the original of the world, and its not being eternal.   25

III. Of a supreme providence in the conservation and goverment of the world.   26

IV. Of that special providence, which in its continued administration about human affaires, doth unchangably difference betwixt the righteus and the wicked.   29

V. How such a wonderful record as that of an immediat revelation of God unto men, is so demonstrably extant in the world.   31

VI. Of these special evidences of the Scriptures divinity, which men must needs see to be infallible.   33

VII. Of the secure convoyance of the Scripture through all the changes of times past.   35

VIII. Of the fall of man and entry of sin into the world, as it is fully demonstrable to reason, as well as by the certainty of faith. 37

SECTION II.

I. Holding fort these great assistances to the Christian faith, and of the Messias being surely promised to the Church before his coming. 38

II. Of the truth and accomplishment of this great promise of the Messias, and how it is now as sure in the event as its clear he was promised. 39

III. Of that special advantage for confirmation of our faith herein, that for 4000. years the promised coming of the Messias was deferred. 41, 42

IV. Of the nature and internal excellency of Christianity, to bear furthest evidence to the truth therof. 43

V. That this is the same Gospel we now receive and injoy, which from the first promulgation therof hath had so great effects on the world. 45

VI. That the sufferings of the saints in times past was so demonstrably above the assistance of nature. 46

SECTION III.

I. For holding forth on what grounds the faith of a deity must determine men to be Christians. 48

II. What confirmations the Christian Religion hath from that visible state of the Jews. 49

III. That way and manner of its prevailing on the world, as no profession else could ever pretend to. 51

IV. The nature of that great evidence, which Christ hath himself given to the world of his divine mission in the love and unity of his people, Joh. 17: 21. 53

V. How the strenth of such a demonstration stands still clear and evident in these dividing times of the Church. 54

VI. What in these last times is under our hand to compense such a confirmation by miracles, which was in the first times of the Gospel. 56

SECTION IV.

I. For holding forth with the furthest rational certainty, and evidence the truth and doctrine of Christ, to be a soul-quickning and experimental religion. 58

II. The truth also of conversion of men from a state of nature to a new state of grace. 60

III. Of so great an experiment of religion as Communion betwixt God and men here in the earth. 62

IV. Of so great a demonstration of religion in the power and workings of the Conscience. 64

V. Of that special confirmation to our faith, which doth result from such a demonstration of this power of the Conscience over men. 65

SEC-

SECTION V.

I. For holding forth the truth of a Kingdom of darknesse in the world, in opposition to the Kingdom of Chrift. 66, 67

II. What confirmation to our faith, the certainty hereof, and of thefe powers of darknesse, doth clearly afford. 68

III. That great truth of the immortality of the foul, with the cleareft evidence to reason, as well as by the certainty of faith. 69, 70

IV. How confirming a feal to the Scripture that great change which paffeth on all men by death is, and how its no natural accident. 72

V. Some fpecial affiftances to the Chriftians faith of an eternal glory in heaven, and to ferve an unavoidable conviction thus on the greateft Atheifts. 74

VI. Some thing of a vifible Hell, in fome near approach hereof even to mens fenfes, held forth to awake and convince the world of fuch a ftate of horrour and torment in another world. 77

VII. Some affiftances to our faith of that great truth of the Refurrection of the body. 79

CHAPTER III.

The Confirming vvorke of religion further improven vvith refpect to this difmal and amazing time vve are novv fallen in.

SECTION I.

To hold forth what may be both for light and confirmation upon this great diftreffe the Churches of Chrift are now under. 81, 82

SECTION II.

How great a talent we ftand accountable for in this day of fuch immediate and extraordinare appearences of the Lord for confirming the fame publick caufe of the Reformed Church fince the Reformation, which we are now called to adhere to. 84

SECTION III.

What manner of time is the prefent lot of the Church now fallen in, and what judgment we ought to have hereof from the Scripture, for our furtheft confirming in fuch a day. 93

SECTION IV.

Some fpecial fervice that we are now called to, and accountable for, in behalf of the truth, and for fanctifying the Lord in the eyes of others, who are under fo great a talent of light and confirmation in the fame. 99

FINIS.

AN IDEA,

*Of the confirm'd state of a Christian in
dismall and shaking times.*

THo the same measure of *Christians*
establishment in the truth be not
alike to all , but must have respect to the different *trialls* , *ta-*
lent , & *improvements* of such for
this end ; yet may it be cause of astonishment,
how rare any study of this kinde is now to be
found , when its not only one of the highest
concerns of *Christianity* , but in a more then ordinary way called for , as the *work of this day;*
yea, that this is a part of religion , which seemes
left improven of any , for the *more gene-*
rall state of professours within the Church ; under some conviction hereof , was this essay de-
signed , where with humble confidence (I may
say) the *truth* hath been sought with that serious enquiry into the *nature of these things* held
forth, as I judged needfull for such, who have
so great ane interest & venture not only through
time , but for all *eternity* , to support upon the
alone certainty hereof , & 'er these *dayes of*
triall, which we now see, passe over this *genera-*
tion , it may be found this was not unseasonable , or without cause directed to such a time,

A   if

if the Lord gracioufly bleffe the fame ; nor will
it (I hope) be found incongruous & without
ufe to prefent yet further , in fuch a method ,
& way of example , fome cleare profpect of
a *confirmed ftate in religion* , & what thefe ought
to be , who with light & affurance of minde
would *follow the Lord fully* , in fuch a day , as
is here offered in a 7 *fold Character* , under
which a *truly confirmed Chriftian in the truth of his
profeßion* may be *ftated.*

CHARACTER. I. That he is one *who hath ane
other fence* , & *impreffion of this great ftudy for
attaining to a confirmed ftate in religion* , & is on
higher grounds preffed to follow the fame , then
*what moft of the vifible Church feemes to appre-
hend* ; & fhould be thus confidred.

1. As one to whom the *glory of the Chriftian profeffion* is in the higheft degree deare , &
to have the world fee , that fuch as embrace
the fame & does moft fully adventure on the
teftimony of God in his word , are thefe alfo
who walks on the higheft principles of true ,
& *enlightned reafon* ; yea , who takes deeply
to heart that obligation which is on all , who
defires to advance the *repute* , & *honor of the
truth* , to be in fuch *tearmes* therewith upon
its *own evidence* , as they may know how to
ferve a rationall conviction both on *Atheifts* ,
& *infidels* , if called thereunto.

2. Who fees alfo , how fuch is the ftate of
falle.

fallen man , as ſtands in need of all the *contri-*
butions that can be , not only to ſtrengthen the
Chriſtians faith , and beare out againſt the ſtrong
aſſaults of *infidelity* , but to gain alſo more credit and *veneration* to the truth with theſe who
are not eaſily delt with , but by ſuch *meanes* ,
as beares ſome *congruity to their naturall light* ,
and reaſon ; for which end the Lord hath af-
foorded theſe miniſteriall helpes , to render the
misbeleefe of the world , or any pretenſe of heſitation about his tru i more fully inexcuſable.

5. He thus ſees , how the moſt important ,
and *fundamentall truths* of Chriſtianity , needs
the greateſt *confirmation of his faith* , & for theſe
who enter in ſo high & diſcriminating a profeſſion from the reſidue of the world , to know
in what manner they embrace the ſame : yea
that the *naturall order of things* does abſolutly require to have the *foundation* ſure laid , on which
ſo great a *ſuperſtructure* muſt reſt , ſo as he
judgeth it a *work by its ſelfe* , and to need ſome
peculiar retiring his ſoul in the moſt ſerious *re-*
ceſſe , and compoſure thereof , to attain *a*
stedfaſtnes of his own in the truth , and to know
the ſtrong and *firm convoyances* of that greateſt
myſtery of the goſpell , in ſuch a manner , as
needes no *paund of a miracle* to confirm the
ſame. But he knowes here that no ſharpneſs of
mens *naturall underſtanding* about the truth can
ever attain a true *reſt* , *and ſettlement of minde*

there-

therein , without a *humble* , and *ferious fpirit*
ftooping doune before the wifedome of God ,
and to enter as *little Children* into his Schoole;
yea that by humble *practice* , and obedience of the gofpell there is ane undoubted comming up to the greateft affurance and *cleareft demonftrations of the fame*, as *Joh; 7: 17.*

4. He knowes that as nothing tends more
to fhake mens fpirits , and ftagger them about
the truth , then a *light and tranfient view* hereof,
fo does the greateft *eftablishment* , follow on
the neareft approach by a *deep and ferious enquiry* about the fame , and thus clearely fees that
if fuch who look but at *a diftance* on the way
of religion , did but once come that length
of triall , as to have their fpirits *feparat* , by
a more ferious reflection thereon , the *firft view*
they fhould have , could not but be matter of
wonder , and amazement , to think what can
determine and fupport in fo marvellous a way as
the life and *practice of Chriftianity* , which is fo
vifibly above nature , and wherein they muft
do violence to the fame , where they muft part
with the *multitude* , and oppofe themfelves to
the ftrongeft tyde *of exemple* , and muft *endure
alfo in hope* , and *believe for things not feen* ,
which were never the object of humane fence ,
to any in this earth , and are oft called to part
with the moft defireable things of *fence* , upon
the alone credit of their *faith* , yea , where
they

they muſt enter in that profeſſion, on no other
tearmes, then to be *martyrs* for the ſame, and
ſeall it with their blood ; ſo that he muſt needs
ſee a Chriſtian according to the *rule* and *in-*
ſtitution of the goſpell, to be the greateſt *riddle*,
and *wonder* of any ſight within time; but when
ſuch come more cloſſe and neare upon this *triall*,
and have once underſtood the *nature* and *great-*
neſſe of that ſecurity which theſe have to adventure on, yea what is the glory of their *hope*,
and the ſure ſpring of their ſupplyes, for their
work and trialls within time, then will this
ſecond wonder unſpeakably exceed the *firſt*; how
its poſſible that ſuch are not of a more *raiſed*,
and *enlarged ſpirit*, in the ſervice of the Goſpell, in that ſhort ſeaſon they have here for
it on the earth, and how their *triall* ſhould
not be more to *beare the joy of ſo great a pro-*
ſpeCt, *and expeCtation*, then any preſent griefes
and troubles, yea how mens life who indeed makes earneſt of the Chriſtian profeſſion,
is not in ſome more continued tranſport of *ra-*
viſhment and wondering, to know that they are
ſurely made for an *eternall ſtate* in another world,
and are among theſe on whom the *glorious God*
hath choiſed to have the exceeding riches of his
grace ſhewed forth in theſe *regions of bleſſedneſs*
above for ever.

5. He hath another ſight and proſpeCt of the
Chriſtian Creed, then moſt who give ane eaſy

aſſent

aſſent thereunto; and hath his reaſon ſo dazeled
with the *revelation of the goſpell* and of the *won-*
ders thereof as hath put him to ſuch ane exer-
ciſe. as that 2 *Chr.* 6: 8. How to credit his eyes
therewith, the more deep reflexion he hath
upon the ſame, *but will God in very deed*
dwell with men on the earth ; and to judge their
caſe, who after ſome fluctuating ſuſpence ,
are admitt to ſee the truth of Chriſtianity, with
that *certainty of its evidence* , as the greatneſs of
ſuch a diſcovery does require , may have ſome
reſemblance to that tranſport which the *Angells*
had at the *firſt being of the creation* , *where the*
morning ſtarres ſung together ; and *the Sonnes of*
God ſhouted for joy, to ſee themſelves thus, who
were brought out of pure nothing, entered into that ineſtable light of ſeeing God , and of
their own bleſſedneſs in him , in ſo high a degree; ſo that he accounts it one of the higheſt
attainements of religion, for a *Chriſtian indeed to*
believe the articles of his own faith , and have
his ſoul thus as fully perſuaded , as of his being , that ſuch a time aſſuredly was , & now
many ages ſince paſt , when the *glorious Redee-*
mer of the Church, the *ſecond perſon of the God head*
came doune from heaven and was revealed in our
nature ; that on him as *ſurety* to divine. juſtice
in the roome of the *Elect* Church, was the
whole *guilt*, and *ſin* thereof transferred , and
in this marvellous way did the holy God *take*.

ſatis-

) himselfe , by himselfe ; that thus
; exalted , by the *incarnation of Chriſt*
ature of *Angels* ; that the time is
he meaneſt afflicted Chriſtian , ſhall
other *aire* , then the breathings of
radiſe above , and now hath ane
oy , and bleſſedneſſe before him ;
a very little time he ſhall know this
ur bleſt Redeemer to his followers
earth , *come ye bleſſed of my father*
Kingdome , &c. when he ſhall take
, and put on the *crown* , when it
t no more a *matter of faith* , but of
artakers of that inheritance with the
it , and know theſe *proper manſi-*
tate of glory and peculiar *aſſignement*
hich all the Redeemed ſhall then
be adjoyned in the ſame claſſe
ct Angels to be as *pure flames* of
oy , yea know what its to walk in
; of the *new Jeruſalem* which are as
nt as Chriſtall , and what that mee-
of his *ſoul perfected* , and in a *tri-*
e with his *glorifyed body* , raiſed in-
nd never to part any more ; and to
oper ſhare of that bleſſed and *great-*
, that ſhall be celebrated in heaven
iage ſupper of the lamb , with the
phant Church , and heare that ho-
ount which the *great judge* will then

A 4   make

make of thefe *trials* of his faith, an(
fli&s which he had gone through w
with that *folemn teftimony of approb*
will be given thereof, and fince it.
great things muft be a part of the *Ch*
can it be ftrange., that fuch, as wo
manner converfe therewith (tho t
yet feen) as no leffe undoubted *re*
any prefent *objects of fenfe*, be not
fyed with a low degree of evidence
mation of their judgement, but that t!
are fure here fhould be perfe&ed fo
ftate of mortality can beare, and the
fy to *rejoyce*, and *glory in tribulati*
weep now for a feafon, who are to
ever, yea to fay in the words of λ:
let them take. it all, & enjoy the
he who is their *life and exceediŋ*
and reignes, who is infinitly bet(
then all thefe things.

6. He accounts the *ftrengthning*
to be fuch a concern, not only as i
venture for all eternity, but as the
of gloryfying God here, that what (
a more full. *confirmation* of the fam
kons alfo one of the greateft *additi*
and comfort within time ; and t!
nyfold *affiftances* with fuch *reduplic*
which the Lord hath himfelfe given
are fuch as no *fragments* of fuch a .

be loft ; & tho he knowes the greateft *demon-ftrations* of our faith can add nothing to the *certainty of divine truth* in it felfe ; yet are they thus given in regard of the ftrong *trials* of a Chriftians life , and of what their *weakneffe* ftand in need of for fupport.

7. Its in this ftudy , he fees and takes to heart , how not only the *condition of man* in the earth , but the *profeffion of Chrift* alfo calls for fuch a reckoning, that he may have *trialls* in that manner difpenfed , when no *vifible refuge* will be found in the leaft to ftand by , but all hu-mane comfort and affiftance wholly to fuccumb; as needes his laying in fuch ballaft now in its feafon , and to be founded thereon with that 'affurance of judgment , as is needfull for that day , when he muft either get through in the alone way of *beleeving* , againft *fence,* or *perish,* and tho no fuch attainments of light can beare out then without prefent and immediat *influen-ces* from above, and that it is fure *according to the day* , *fo muft the Chriftian ftrength be* , yet does he fee alfo , the want of ane eftablifhed judge-ment , and of fome *proper ftock* laid up of *aides* , and *affiftances* this way forgainft a fharpe ftorm , is like to make *fad work among the pro-feffours of this age* , er the trialls of fuch a time have done their work.

8. He fees alfo how the greateft *conteft* , which is this day in the world , is *betwixt God* , and

man,

man , upon the *truth and assurance of his word*; and that the highest *triall* , and *probation of a Christian* , in which all the trialls of their life does still meet , may be resolved here , if they receive *the testimony of God* in his word as an *absolute security* to rely on , yea or not , and tho this is the peculiar glory of the *only true God* , to have ane absolute *dependance* of his whole work on himselfe ; and to be the *alone center of his peoples rest*, yet may nothing be more evident, then that with most he beares that name , of *being their trust* ; when the whole burden and weight thereof lyes alone upon visible grounds , so that those *bonds* , *and promises* which he hath himselfe given unto men does beare no more credit , then they have some *externall surety in the earth* , which they still looke after , to stand as it were good and *responsible* for the same , which is the highest *indignity* can be offered to the glorious Majesty of God.

9. He does much take to heart this *present period of time* , wherein the fluctuating suspence and *halting* of so many under a visible profession of the truth is now one of the most dismall signes hereof; & that it seemes to be the *time*, wherein the Lord will in ane unusuall way take this generation off any *implicit profession* of the same ; and when that *great roll of visible professours* in all the *reformed* Churches may be er long in that manner *called*, as each must *answer*

to *his own name* , and put to ftand to the *proofe* before the world , when no temporall intereft, but *internall motives* and certainty of the truth upon its own *evidence* , muft beare out ; yea that the moft *eftablisht* may er long finde it not eafy to be keept from ftaggering , and a few dayes come in the Churches way , more remarkable for *triall* then hath been in fome *ages* before.

CHARACT. II. *A truely confirmed Chriftian*, may be thus alfo ftated as one who is in the *firft place* moft deeply taken up about that *rare plot of mans redemption* , and to fee thefe *great and wonderfull truths there*, *not fingly* , and *apart*, but in that *harmony*, *order* and *confent of all the parts thereof* , as *they are linkt together in this marvellous frame* , *fo as to make the whole one entire peece*, and where no part does in the leaft interfere with an other , which he finds to be one of the moft *principall demonftrations* of this great myftery of the Gofpell, that the Lord hath given for *confirming* his peoples faith ; and thus in another manner then formerly can now entertain his foul herewith , and have his joy unfpeakably hightned , 1 to fee at once the *ruined ftate of fallen man* , and what a floodgate of all evill is let loofe on that race, not only *morally in fin* , but what is *penall* in the *woe* and miferyes thereof ; yea fuch a ftate , where all hope of releefe is for ever cut off in the way of nature or by any created help ; and where

the

the execution of a *righteous sentence* on such for
the voluntare violation of a *law* , *juft, holy* and
equall , can be no impeachment in the leaft
of the *righteoufnefs of God* ; But then therewith
he does fee fuch a releefe brought to light as
can not only anfwer the whole extent of this ruin,
but the *glory of God* more eminently difplayed therin , then if the *law* had been *obeyed* , or *abfolu-
tely execute* in its *penalty* on the whole race of man,
yea which makes this more wonderfull to fee a
higher *difpenfation of grace* unto man now under
the gofpell then was to *Adam in his primitive ftate* ;
whereby innumerable Chriftians are made to endure and prevail over *ftronger affaults* then broke
him even in his *integrity* , which is a conjunction fo marvellous that the great and infinit God
only could finde out and effectuat. 2. He
does now fee how cleare a confiftence and harmony is here , that he who had no fin by *in-
hefion* , but holy, harmles, and undefiled, fhould
be under the greateft weight of fin by *imputation*
and by the exacteft rule of divine juftice made
liable to anfwer both the whole *duty* , *and full
penalty of the Law* , having as *furety* betwixt the
creditor & *debter,* put himfelfe in his peoples roome
to anfwer the full demands thereof both for
debt , *aud duty.* 3. It is here he does fee that
bleft confent and harmony betwixt the fpot-
les *juftice of God* , and his marvellous *grace* , fo
as his *love* is to the higheft glorifyed , in that marvellous

(13.)

vellous way , as fecures the full and compleat
fatisfaction of his *Law* , and all the rights of *juftice* inviolable. 4. Whilft he is thus dazled with
the greatnes of fuch a light , and put to enquire
what fuch a myftery can mean , he is then fur-
der led on to fee that *rare plot* and contrivance
of the *covenant of reconciliation* between God and
man , here within time to be the very *duplicat*,
and *counterpart* of that eternall tranfaction and *fti-
pulation between the father and the fon*; and thus
fees what ever God hath declared and *promifed*
in the *one* to his Church , was firft *promifed and
fecured to our bleffed head in the covenant of Redemption* ; wherein as with a reverend and awfull diftance , fo with the greateft evidence of
light he is made to fee here thefe reciprocall *obligations* betwixt them , and *mutuall truft* for making good the whole tearmes thereof in the ap-
poynted time. 5. He does alfo clearly fee that
rare *order* & *harmony* of time in thefe *fignall periods*
of the revelation of this great myftery of Chrift
which from its more dark difcovery and dawning
did ftill more glorioufly open its felfe to the *Church*
by a *graduall light* and unvailing of the fame,as the
Sun in its courfe unto the perfect day; yea hath his
faith thus unfpeakeably confirmed to fee herewith
the *gofpell* Church being ftill the fame , whither
of *Jewes* or *Gentil's* , and how that *feries* and *confent* hath yet never been broken off fince the beginning of *one* Church feparat from the refidue
of

of mankinde fet apart as a peculiar people for the
Lord, where none ever had right and priviledge
to be members of the fame, but by *faith in the
Meffias*, and profeffion of their obedience to his
Lawes. 6. It is in this *union and harmony* he fees
the whole branches and parts of gofpell obedience
moft exactly meet, and terminat, to advance
both the greateft excellency and *bleffednefs of man*,
and *affimulat* him to the *bleffed image of God*, yea
how all the rules and precepts there does fo entir-
ly confpire for this end as may conftrain the
world to fee, and admire the *glorious nature*,
and *perfections of him*, whofe lawes thefe are,
wherein he does fo brightly fhine forth. 7. Nor
can he looke ferioufly herein and not fee that fweet
concord as a part of this *harmony*, which is betwixt
the *promiffory*, *and mandatory part of the gofpell*,
fo as the Chriftians comfort is moft fully eftablifhed and no duty abolifhed; but the very path rod
to the muft full enjoyments of the promife and
proper way to attain reft and tranquillity of fpirit
muft be ever here by taking on the yoke of Chrift.
8. Yea to confirm this entire union and harmony more fully he now fees that exact and marvellous correfpondence which is betwixt that firft
fundamentall promife of the *Meffias*, and the *event*;
betwixt the whole ancient *figures and types* of
the *leviticall fervice* and the revelation of *Chrift
himfelfe*, in which all thefe did meet as their
proper *center*, and now have their full end and

accom-

accomplishment. 9. His confirmation thus grows to see that wonderful confent of *Chriftianity*, and native refult hereof to put fallen man in a due *poftour towards God*, towards his *neighbour*, and *himfelfe*, fo as he may know by *faith* and *adoration* how to *enjoy God*, and his *brother* by *love*, and thus by *patience*, *meeknes* and *humility* to *poffeffe his own foul*, and enjoy himfelfe. 10. Yea it is in this rare and wonderfull frame he is made to fee (and no fight can be like this) that exact correfpondence which is betwixt the *foundation* and *fuperftructure*, how the whole *tract of the gofpell* is but one entire and compleat *mean to glorify God*, and *reftore fallen man* to the higheft bleffednes, how that excellent ftream of *fanctification* does flow from that fountain head of ane eternall decree herein, which does ftill run under the ground, until it *break up* at laft in the heart of each Chriftian, by the *effectuall call of the gofpell*; and thus runs doune through time untill it lofe its felfe in that unconceiveable deep of *perfection* and *glory*. Thus is it that each Chriftian might attain fome higher degrees of *confirmation* in *his faith*, then moft feemes either to know or looke after if he underftood more how to improve this rare *comparing work of Religion* by fetting the great truths and principles thereof in their order & dependance fo as each may be feen, in its neceffare *coherence* with other, and under its *proper afpect*.

But the more deep reflexion and enquiry he
                                 hath

hath herein, he is the more made to wonder and finds this one of the great affaults to his faith, that the *revelation of the Chrift, and redemption by his blood should have no greater effects this day* amongft men, and that the *Chriftian world* is not in fome other manner awaked with the *glory* of this light, and preft after a larger fpreading and *diffufion* of this *higheft* and *univerfall good* to poore man-kinde; yea the more he confiders this it doth highten his amazement to think how mens de-figns in the matter of duty and fervice for the Kingdome of Chrift, can be fo *low* within time, whofe *defigns* and *hopes* in the clofe therof are fo *high* in the matter of *enjoyment*; or take fo litle to heart, that the whole *day of the difpenfation of the Gofpell*, amidft the moft difmal trials may fall in therewith, is a continued time wherein we are called *to keep the feaft*, and from one age to an-other celebrate the fame, as a perpetuall *Jubily of joy and exultation*, fince *Chrift our paffover was facrificed for us*; but oh how rare a thing feems this to be, and how litle of that flame and fervency of *love to our bleffed Redeemer is now kindled on his altar*, that might be expected on fuch wonde rfull incitments therto, and which once was in the Church.

CHARACT.III. Though a *confirmed Chrifti-an* muft be fpecially ftated as fuch, who *knowes the internall part of religion, and fealing work of the Holy Ghoft* on his own foul, which is not by *words*,

but

but *things* of the higheſt *truth*, *ſubſtance*, and *rea-lity*; yet is he herein not alone ſatisfyed to know this by *ſpirituall ſence*, untill he can ſee the ſame with the furtheſt *evidence of light* alſo to his mind; and have no leſſe a clear and *judicious tryal* of this great myſterie of *experimentall religion*, for con-firmation of his faith, then to be *ſenſibly* affected with the felt power therof. And in the *firſt place* why this is neceſſarly requiſite and called for, with reſpect to the *confirmed ſtate* of a Chriſtian, may be thus *conſidered*, on ſome *few grounds*.

1. That the things of religion, which muſt be *experienced* within time, are ſuch ſublime, and *wonderfull myſteries*, as may be juſt matter of aſtoniſhment, and make men a wonder to themſelves, to think that theſe preſent *pledges* of ſo great a hope which is to come, are no *ſhaddows*, no appearences of things, but moſt ſure and undoubted *realities*; and that ſuch are this day in the earth who knowes ſo near a con-verſe with an *inviſible God*, and the *ſupernaturall truths* of his word, with the ſenſible fealing of that *ineſtimable love of Chriſt*, by this demonſtration of *experience*; yea who in ſuch diſmall times does aſſuredly know what the *joy of his preſence*, and an immediate fellowſhipe with their bleſſed head is, upon the greateſt certainty of tryal; ſince theſe are ſo high, and marvelous things, which exceed all *naturall underſtanding*, as the *felt ſweet-neſſe* of their enjoyment ſhould not more deeply

B take

take men up , then to fee the *truth* , and *furenesse* of *thefe principles* , wheron they found herein.

2. Becaufe this teftimony of the truth of *experimentall religion* , fhould be underftood not only as its of higheft ufe for Chriftians *perfonall comfort* and eftablifhment , but with refpect to the *publick intereft* of the Church , as a fpecial truft repofed theron , to have the *credit* of this greateft teftimony and *feal* , *demonftrably cleared,* with the furtheft ftrength of *harmonious, and argumentive reafon* , for fuch who look but at a diftance yet theron , as may not only awake them to fome deeper *fenfe* and impreffion hereof , but conftrain them to fee , how no *naturall fcience* hath more clear , and firm *demonftrations,* then the *experimentall'part of Chriftiani-ty,* (which is the very life and foul thereof,) may have to mens *reafon* , and *judgement* , tho they never knew it within themfelves ; yea for this end fhould fuch , as have experienced the *truth,* and *vertue of the Gofpell* , reckon themfelves as *witneffes* who are *judicially fifted to put their feal* therunto; & is now more called for in an age,when no particulare truth feems more ftrongly impugned , then the *reality of experimental godlineffe* is, and become as a *publick theam of derifion* , tho men muft either quite the whole revelation of the Scripture , or fee this to be as *effentiall to the conftitution of a Chriftian* , as *vitall principles* are to a *living man.*

3. Yea

3. Yea its fure herein , that fuch as take religion to heart , muſt needs look to be put
to the *greateſt tryal of its certainty*, and ſhould moſt
nearly concern them to know if they can *abide
as firmly by their ſpirituall ſenſe* as by that which
is *naturall*, and doe thus know as ſurely in themſelves the *operations and motions of a ſpirituall life*,
as that they have being by *nature* ; and that here
is no doubtfull or abſtract notions , but who
have had ſuch deep *tryall and reflexion* on the
ſame as theſe who dare venture their *eternal ſtate*
on the known certainty therof, as they could thence
reaſon their ſoul to a ſtedfaſt adherence to the
truth , if they were called to *ſacrifice their lives*
therto, from what *rare experiments*, and *proofs*,
they have oft had of the ſame in their own *tryall*.

4. It doth more ſpecially call for a demonſtrative clearing of the credit of this teſtimony,
as one of the *ſervices of religion* , to promote
the Kingdom of Chriſt amonghſt men , which
ſeems leaſt *improven* of any with reſpect to the
general ſtate of ſuch who are within the Church,
who are ſo great ſtrangers to the ſame ; yea
ſhould be judged one of the *great wants* of this
day , when Atheiſm is now at ſo aſtoniſhing a
hight , that it is not more ſtudied to have the
experimentall part of religion , (which in it ſelf
lyes deep and hid, and is a ſecret betwixt God
and the Chriſtians ſoul ,) with ſuch *clearneſſe*,
and by that *manner of evidence* demonſtrat to

the

the world , as might tend to beget fome more *awfull fenfe* and conviction hereof, (when fuch clear and unanfwerable grounds might be improved for this end) on thefe who look thereon as fome ftrang and dark riddle , fo as they could no more deny or withftand the *evidences* hereof, then that they have a *living foul which yet they never faw*, or could ever be the object of human fenfe. And how fad a profpect fhould this give of the greateft part of the *Chriftian world*, who not only know nothing of the *true glory* , and *fpirituall powers of Chriftianity*, but have not the very *notion* , or any *fenfe* of the reality of fuch a thing.

But in the 2d *place* it is thus that each Chriftian, for being folidly confirmed in the way of religion , may as *clearly fee* , as he does *fenfibly feal*, the truth of his own experience, and have his faith as fully eftablifhed by this *inward* and *great demonftration* of the things of God , as his *affections are quickned* , upon fuch ftrong and *demonftrative grounds* of the *certainty* hereof , as thefe are.

1. By *confidering* , his *prefent* and *former ftate* , that not in a dream , but in the moft deep and ferious compofure of fpirit , he knows how *once he was blind* and wholly eftranged from this myfterie of *Chriftian experience* , which now he does fee ; and once had the fame *fentiment* hereof with fuch who doe moft deeply reflect on the fame , but no fooner did the truth , and

power

power of religion seafe on his foul ; then he found himfelf *entered into a new world* to know the dawnings of this *marvelous light* , and what belongs to thefe injoyments , and *vital acts* of Chriftianity , that hath not the leaft dependence on any *naturall caufe.*

2. By confidering that *marvelous fuperftructure of experimentall religion* , which from the *inward obfervation of Chriftians in all ages* , is fuch as the *world could not* almoft *contain the books , that might be write hereof* , which yet is fo intirely founded on one and the *fame foundation*, and does in all the *lines* of this great *circumference* , ftill meet in the *fame center* ; yea thus how intire and *harmonious* a thing religion in all the parts therof is *within* upon the foul , as well as *without,* fo as every *ftep in this way* of the *experience* of the faints is no groping in the dark, but what is by *line* and *rule* , with as fure and demonftrable a connexion with the *externall teftimony of the word*, as there is in *nature* betwixt the *caufe* and the *effect* ; which affords a more wonderfull affiftance to his faith , then the greateft *externall miracles* could ever doe; and tho the fpirit of God does fometimes in an *extraordinare manner* reveal himfelf to men (as *acts of his Soveraign prerogative* which make no *rule*) yet with the eftablifhed *conftitutions of his word* does the continued experience of the faints moft harmocioufly ever *correfpond.*

3. By considering thus also the *being*, & *re-ality of grace* , not in its *effects* only but in its *proper cause and original*, & how the *truth of holinesse* in the life of a Christian is so expres a transcript of the Gospell, in its *external reve-lation* , that the *impresse* doth not more clearly answer *the seal on the wax* then it doth beget the same *forme and image of it self* in such as *believe*; yea also that conformity it bears to the *ever blessed Architype* , *as well* as to the *revealed ru-le* , and how bright a discovery is thus of so *glorious a being* , *and nature*, to which its con-formed , who is the alone *patern* , and *exemple of all truth and holinesse* ; which is so great a discovery , as he is made to wonder , how men in this age are so much awakened to find out the *true Phænomena of nature* , (though in its own room a most choise study , and specialy desirable,) and will be as in a *transport* , upon some rare *natural experiment* , as made one in that manner cry out εὑρῆκα εὑρῆκα; whilst here is another kind of *demonstration* ; and of more transcendent interest then all these could ever amount to, on which the eyes of most are this day shutt.

4. By considering that *uncheangable congruity*, *which is betwixt the nature of these things , injoy-ned in the whole institutions of the Gospell* , and *mens being made happy therby* , now in their pre-sent state , and how great a temporal revenew

of

of the fruits of religion , as inward *confidence* , *peace* , and *ferenity of mind* , doth as natively fol-low the life and practice herof , as the *fruit* of *a tree* anfwers to its *kind* , and is ever found the alone *true relief of mankind* , againft all the griefs and bitterneſſe of time ; yea that its no *diſtance of place* , but of *mens fpirit* by *impurity* , and cor-ruption that makes fo fad a diſtance betwixt God, and man here in the earth.

5. He is thus further confirmed upon this great *teſtimony of experimentall religion* , by confi-dering that its fure fuch as does bear this witneſſe are known ; 1. to be fuch who are of the moſt *difcerning and judicious* in the things of *reaſon* , as any elfe. 2. Whofe *walke* and *practice* ufe to have the greateſt authority over mens confcience with whom they converfe. 3. who are found moſt intenſly taken up in the *retired worke* , *and duties of religion* , that can have no refpect to the witneſſe and obfervation of others. 4. Who feeks no *implicit credit* from any herein , but does ob-teſt men to *come and fee* , and prove the fame in their their own *experience* , with an *appeal* to the moſt exact inquiry , and *rationall tryall* of all mankind, if here be any *cafuall thing,* and if that teſtimony of the *doctrinall,* and *experimentall part* of religion be not ſtill one and the fame. 5. Who alfo out of the moſt *remott places* of the earth , and otherwife ſtrangers amonghſt themfelves , does yet moſt harmonioufly meet in the *fame wit-neſſe,*

neſſe , and are thus *mutually diſcloſed to other* , by a near and fealing intercourſe of their ſouls , from ſuch an *onneſſe in a ſpirituall ſtate* and theſe *ſpecifick-properties* of a ſpirituall , and *new nature,* with as diſcernible evidence as if one *man* ſhould meet with ane other of the *ſame kind* , in ſuch a place of the earth which were only inhabited with *beaſts.*

6. By conſidering alſo , (with a deep and ſe-rious reflection hereon ,) that ſure and known *conjunction* , which is betwixt the moſt *rare ex-periences* of a Chriſtians life , and the moſt *ſe-arching tryalls* thereof , with that uniform con-ſent , that hath in all ages of the Church been, in ſuch marvelous things , as theſe. 1 what *ſolemne tokens and teſtimonies of the love of God,* and his *acceptance* , are found uſually to meet his people in the *entry* of ſome great *tryall,* or *ſervice* for him , even in ſome unuſuall manner then , in *the ſence whereof,* as it was with *Eli-jah,* they have been made to *goe many days af-ter in a wilderneſſe ſtate*; yea how this does not reſpect *perſons* only , but *Churches,* that the word ſtill uſeth to goe before with ſome remarkable *confirming worke* to ſecure the heart , before the *croſſe* and ſome ſpecial tryal of *perſecution* comes 2. That as each day hath its *proper burden* , and worke , ſo hath it its *proper allowance* provided for the ſame , which ſhould be no leſſe ſought after by a Chriſtian , then his *dayly bread,* and

when

when the preffure of fuch a day grows to fome more fingulare hight , fo alfo fhould the expenfe hereof be in faith fought for & expected. 3. How the *choifeft mercies* are referved to the *faddeft times* of a Chriftians lot , and moft ufually croffe to their own *choife*, and thus hath had the greateft ftruglings with thefe *methods of providence* , which hath in the iffue tended moft to their upmaking. 4. Yea how the returnes of a *long deferred hope* after much humble on-waiting, have been to fuch as a *Pisgah*, whence they have not only had a clear and comforting *profpect of their bypaft tryals*, but for being more fully confirmed of the *time to come* ; and can bear now that teftimony, *that the Lord hath cleared all bygones to them* , and hath taken *the vail off his worke* , which for long had been as a dark and ftrang riddle.

7. This likeways gives a moft clear, and confirming profpect of that great *feal of experience*, when he can now fee , both in his own cafe and of others, what the *issue of believing in a fingular exigence and tryal* and upon fome fpecial act of *truft and adventure herein does at laft come to* ; which the more deeply its confidered he finds one of the moft peculiare *affiftances to his faith* , and one of the *greateft attainments of experimentall religion* within time , when he can thus fee the fame way of *believing*, (in fome ftrong and extraordinare affaults , which he hath had to

B 5

cruſh

crufh and break him herein ,) which hath car-
ried fo many thorow in their faddeft tryals , bring
him alfo in *his turn*, to be an *inftance in the fame
kind*, to bear an honourable *teftimony* to this
fure, and *excellent way of believing before the world*,
and that none fear , *after him* , to *hold by the
promife of God* and venture on that fecurity , tho
it then feem againft hope , whofe *difpenfations* ,
did yet never , never give his word the lye.

· C H A R A C T. IV. Such is a truely *confirmed Chriftian, who in a difmall time* , *is not
ftaggered in his faith from the prefent figns and appearences therof* , but hath his *foul ballaft with
fuch folid grounds of confirmation* againft the fame,
as thefe *providences,* wherat others doe moft *ftum-
ble,* tends to his further *ftrenthning in the way of
the Lord* , when he does now clealy *fee*;

1. How *tribulation and the croffe* makes one
of the moft *illuftrious and beutifull parts* of the
whole frame of providence about the *Church* , and
in the lot of each Chriftian; fo as there can be
no poffible *ftumbling* to any for want of light
here, that fore *tryalls*, and *diftreffe* fhould moft
remarkably follow thefe in their *journey* , who
have an *eternall bleffedneffe* before them in the
clofe hereof, when fo great a part of the *Scripture* is directed not only for *comfort* but for a
clear *conduct of the Chriftians faith* , through all
the *intrcacies* and *labyrinths* of fuch a difpenfation , and thus fees how highly *congruous* it is
to the

to the infinit wifdom of God , that fo *ftrait and narrow a way* , in fuch a *ftate of tryall* as is here, fhould goe before the ftate of everlafting injoyment ; that there fhould be fuch a *ftage* and *theatre* alfo , whereon the *paffive graces of the fpirit* , may not only be *exercifed* , but *difplayed in their true luftre* and *glory before Angels and men* ; yea that thus the Redeemed of the Lord be firft *trained* in fo fharp a *warfare* , as may not only put a *due value* and *refpect* on the greatnefs of that *triumph* and *reward* which is to come, but be matter of *ineffable joy and exultation* , that ever they were admitt thus to evidence their love and adherence to their *bleffed head* and his *truth* here on the earth , and accounted *worthy* to be put on fome *hotter fervice* , and to peculiare *tryals* and *conflicts* this way beyond others , for fome *example* and incouragement to the *Church in their day* ; and here alfo he can now fee how the greateft *injoyments of comfort* are more oweing to the moft fharp and *afflicting tryals* of their life, then to the greateft *externall calme* ; and that to *endure* patiently and *fuffer for the name Chrift* is fuch a priviledge as the *elect Angels* have not been admitt to , yea that the Lords *chaftning worke*, and foreft *fmitting* of his own , is *an act alfo of faving* ; fo that thus the more deeply he fearcheth here , the more does he *fee, admire,* and *confent* to that *glorious piece of the adminiftration of providence* about the Church , and finds it to it to be one of the greatest *confirmations of his* *faith* within time.

2. He does now clearly fee how the *truth* and *faithfu'neſſe* of *God is commenſurate to his whole worke of Providence* & that all the *lines* hereof , as they doe lead from his revealed councell in the *Scripture*, which is the *adequat ſigne* of his *eternall councell and decrees* , ſo doe they returne thither again , to make this great *demoſtration* clear ; that if a *full Hiſtory were write of this world* , and what hath been conspicuous thorow the whole ſeries of times paſt in all theſe conjunctions of *inferiour cauſes* , whether *neceſſare* , *free* , or *contingent* , and of ſuch events that ſeem moſt *caſual* , it ſhould be nothing elſe but an exact transcript and *hiſtory of the Bible,* to bear this witneſſe , *quod mundus nihil aliud eſt quam Deus explicatus ſecundum ſcripturam;* but though a full diſcovery hereof be not attainable within time , yet is it a ſad and deplorable want , that the *great acts of the Lord,* in each *age* of the Church are not more ſearched *and ſought out of all them that take pleaſure therin,* that they may be *ſeen,* *obſerved* , and *admired* by that part of the creation, *Angels* and *Men* , who are only in a capacity to know the ſame ; which is a ſervice for the Lord wherin his *praiſe* , and *declavative glory* is ſo highly conceirned, as a Chriſtian ſhould account the meaneſt *roome* herein one of the moſt deſirable attainments within time; yea it

seems

seems juft matter of regret alfo that this comes not under a more *publick care* and nottice of *particulare Churches and* of the *Chriftian Magiftrate*, where religion hath any true regard, to have fuch *folemne providences* as occurre in that *time*, and *place*, which may be called *experimenta lucifera to the Church*, and of a further reach and extent then any private ufe, both *fearch'd* after and *recorded* as becomes fo high a *fervice to the Chriftian caufe* and one of rhe higheft conceirns of the *pofteritie*, to have fuch not only poffeffed of a pure *religion*, but of that *feal* alfo; which the Lord hath in the *great acts* of providence *appended* therto, and thus to have that *increafe*, which each fucceffive age brings therwith to the *publick ftock of the Church*, looked after, as a piece of the greateft truft repofed theron, fo that the Children rife not up and fay, we have not *heard nor have our fathers faithfully tranfmitt* to us the *wonderous works which the Lord hath wrought in their time.*

3. He is thus alfo tought to fee the δίοτι and *demonftrative caufes* of the moft ftrang judgments on the Church, to be as *clear in the Scripture* as they are in the *event*, and though the holy God in the day of his *patience*, and *longfuffering* is not alike quick in the execution of the *fentences* of his word, yet does he ever eftablifh the *authority of his Laws* by the *works* of his *providence* in the moft opportune feafon; and

and as *judgment deferred* , is no *acquittance* , so
does it more threaten its being the *greater* ,
when it comes , then a *quick and present dis-*
patch ; yea though this *tempest* which now blowes
on the Churches of Christ , come to a greater hight , and the darknesse be such, as *no Moon*
or *Starres* may for many dayes yet appear of
any *visible signs of hope* , yet is his soul thus at
rest whilst he can see the *credit of the truth clea-*
red , on which he hath more in *dependence* then
any *adventure* within time, and does rejoyce ,
whatever miscarrying may be of inferiour *ends* ,
that this great and *ultimate end* of the works of
God is secured herein , and the *glory of his truth*
does shine forth in the most strang and *amazing*
acts of his providence , wherat many are ready to
stagger , when they doe not *wisely* consider the
same.

4. He sees now likewise , so *high a value*
which the Lord puts on the tryall of his peoples faith ,
and that the great dispensation wherby he deales
with men is *by trust* and on the *credit of his*
word , as it addes further to his confirmation ,
to see all human and *visible refuges* oft taken out
of his Churches sight ; yea his *greatest works*
in the earth make the *greatest delay* er they be
brought forth , & his Churches case put so far
beyond help before a *cure* , as the first quickning of her crushed and allmost *dead hope* , must
be at the *mouth of the grave* ; and he is thus here-

in more fingularly ftrenthned , that when the
Lord fpeaks the fame in the *way of prov dence*,
which he hath fpoke in his word , *not by might
nor by power* , that he doth with unspeakable
advantage *fupply* and *fill the roome* therof by the
next word , *but by my fpirit faith the* Lord ,
which in this day fhould with a *full affurance
of faith* be both fought and looked after.

5. It is in this rare *ftudy* he attaines alfo the
greateft *confirmation* to his faith that could poffibly be defired within time, to fee now when
its fo near the *clofe* therof and after all the revolutions of times paft , how the *truth and
fa thfu''neffe of God* , hath , as the fun in its
ftrenth , ftill keept its way ftraight and fixt a-
midft all thefe dark clouds which have been to
darken the fame and is now gone its courfe untill it draws near to the full and perfect day;
yea thus to fee how *fignally this prefent age is fifted
upon that fame appeal* and folemne *teftimony* which
as *Jofua* gave , *Jofh. 23: 14. that not one thing
hath failed of all the good things which the Lord
your God fpake concerning yow , all are come to
paffe to yow , and not on thing hath failed thereof* ; and *Solomon* did bear alfo at the *dedication* of the
Temple , 1 *Kings* 8: *v.* 56. *Bleffed be the Lord
that hath given reft unto his people Ifrael , according
to all that he promifed , there hath not failed one word
of all his good promife , which he promifed by the hand
of Mofes his fervant* ; fo is this now that great *teftimony of the latter dayes* and the higheft *tribute* of
praife to the glory of God in his truth which can be
given

given by men , that this prefent generation
ftands accountable to make the fame yea much
greater appeal to the world , if they can inftance one *promife* or *prediction* of that facred record of the Scripture which hath ever failed
or fallen to the ground , but may be *this day
read in the event*, & under thefe proper *circumftances* wherin it was to take place in its
proper feafon , as evidently as it was *fortold* ,
and muft ftill bear the fame witnes , Pfa!, 18 :
30. *that the way of the Lord is perfect* , and *his
word tryed* on all the *adventures of faith* , and
tryals which to this moment of time have been
made hereof, and of his being ftill a *buckler* to
fuch as truft in him, and are called to transmitt
this glorious *teftimony* to the fucceeding *ages*, that
it may never ceafe to *fhine* or want a publick
witneffe therto before *Angels* and *men* , untill
the *whole myftery* of God *in his word be finifhed*
in that magnificent clofe which fhall be therof
at the *fecond coming of the Lord.*

CHARACT. V. A *confirmed Chriftian* in
this day fhould be thus alfo *ftated* , as one who hath
not only attained a *folid reft* and *fettlment of
m'nd* , upon the *certainty of the Chriftian faith* ,
but does know the *pure genuine truth of Chriftian'ty* , amidft fuch high oppofitions betwixt the
Romish and *Reformed Church* herein.

And in the 1 place hath in this *manner* fifted
himfelf upon fuch a *tryal*; 1 as one who knows
there

there is but one *true* and *saving religion* in the earth, to which God hath annexed the promise of *eternall life* which can never be divided against it self. 2. Who knows that within a litle his *religion will be tryed* in the truth therof at the *tribunall of Christ* , where each must *give account of himself unto God.* 3. As such who sees there can be no possible *indifference* in the *exterior profession* of either way , but that so high a contrariety of principles is in this *opposition* , that if the *doctrine of Christ* be on the one hand , it is sure *Antichristianisme* must be on the other hand. 4. Yea who hath in that *abstract manner* sought to *state the case* herein with his own soul as if he were come out of *Paganism* , to give a serious assent to the *divinity of the Scripture* , and thus pressed to joyn in with that profession of the *Christian faith* , which is most exactly conforme to the same , in the *genuine* and *perspicuous fence* therof.

In the *2d place* he hath sought to know, how he could imbrace the *Popish creed* and adventure his eternall state theron, or can extinguish his *reason*, and *conscience* so far as to believe that the *holy God would ever impose such a faith upon men , as this is*; 1 where he must abandon these principles of *naturall reason* in the most necessare use therof , which God hath himself *planted* in mans soul , so as not to *trust* his *own eyes* but others in that great interest of his *eternall state* , and

with his own confent be fhutt out from all proper knowledge of the *rule* of his religion , yea
account a *blind* and *unlimited obedience to men* ,
amongft the higheft *excellencies of faith.* 2. Where
he muft at once believe the *fullneſſe* , and *perfection of the Scripture* , and to be not only fitted
for that great end of *bringing mankind to God* ,.
but for fuch an *univerſall uſe* herein , as to make the
ſimple wiſe, and that the *poor may receive the Goſpell;*
and yet believe alfo that it is a *maſſe of dead* ,
and unſenſed characters , untill the Romiſh Cler-
gy put a juft *ſenſe* theron , tho its *ſenſe* and mean-
ing is the very *ſoul* thereof , yea thus paſſe from
the whole *letter* of the fame, or any certainty of its
truth ; from *intrinſick evidences* and thefe *marks*
and *characters of its divinity* , wherby the Chriſ-
tian cauſe could be maintain'd againft Pagans. 3.
Where he muft believe alfo that thefe are the
words of Chrift *Joh. 7: 17. if any man doe my
will he shall know my doctrine whither it be of God or
not,* and that men *errs through not knowing the Scripture
Math. 22.* and yet believe therewith , that thefe
ſacred fountains of light should *be shutt up , to keep men
from going wrong* , and that the fole right of un-
derftanding the fame belongs to a *few* , but not
to the *multitude* , who yet can pretend no extraordinare *aſſiſtance or revelation* herein , nor
will themfelves come to thefe *waters of Jealouſie
to be tryed.* 4. Where he muft needs believe
that the Scriptures are the *oracles of God committ*

to the Church , to give anſwer in every darke
caſe Rom. 3: 2. the *type and forme of ſound do-*
ctrine , Rom. 6. 17. unto whoſe *ſentence* in all
matters both of *faith and practiſe* , we are expreſly referred , Iſ. 8. 20. and yet *believe* alſo that it hath no *authority* or *deciſive voice* , but
what is *precarious* and dependant on the Romiſh
Church , and thus conſent to have the whole
Chriſtian faith *viſibly unhinged* of that *foundation of*
the Scripture , and ſubjected to a *ſupreme, viſi-*
ble , and *infallible judge* here in the earth , with
ſuch a claime of *dominion over the faith of the*
ſaints , as the *Apoſtles of* Chriſt durſt never owne,
but did fully diſclaime 2 Cor. 1: 24. 5. Where
he muſt believe that *Jeſus* Chriſt came for
this end, to *ſave loſt man* , and by one *offering hath*
perfected for ever them that are ſanctified Heb. 10: 18.
and yet joyn in the ſame faith herewith a *hu-*
man ſatisfaction for ſin, ſo as men may both me-
rit , *mediate* , and *ſupererogate* above what is
needfull for themſelves, and be thus ſaved in the
ſame *way of life ;* which was by the *covenant of*
works; aſcribing that only to Chriſt to give ſalvation to their *merits* , which yet their own *in-*
trinſick value , and *condignity* doth require as a
debt. 6. He finds not how in the ſame
creed he could poſſibly hold by *one Mediator be-*
twixt God and man, where a *plurality* for this
end is admitt ; and by the reality of Chriſts *hu-*
man nature , and his having a true and *finit bo-*

dy , which is fubjected to have a *new created being* , each time in the *Confecrate Hoftia* ; or believe the truth of his *fufferings* as now fully accomplifhed , and to be *repeated* no more , when· it is in that *dayly facrifice of the Mef-fe ftill offered* , as a *propitiatory facrifice for the liveing and the dead*; fo as on the moft fevere and im-partial inquiry here , he cannot find how one holding by thefe *principles*fhould goe a further lenth then *Morality* , or claim another ftanding then by a *covenant of works.* 7. Nor knows he how to believe at once the truth of the *Gofpell*, to be a *doctrine of Holineffe* , and *infinite purity* , and yet joyne in the fame *faith* herewith fuch an *immunity and indulgence* for men to *fin* , as *mo-ney* can ftand for *merit*, and the *rich* have the moft *eafy* and *large entrey* to heaven and ac-count it a *priviledge to deftroy themfelves*; yea where fome externall *feverities* and pennance to the flefh , like to the *lanching* and *gafhing of Baals Priefts* , are reckoned enough to fupply the roome of *Chriftian mortification.* 8. Yea he finds it not pofible to *believe* , that *fin* by the *blood of Chrift can only· be expiate*, and is his alone worke, who hath *purged our fin himfelf, Heb.* 1: 3. or that there are but *two ways* that lead to a *twofold ftate* of men , a *ftrait* way which leads to a *life*, and a *broad* unto *deftruc-tion* , *Math.* 7: 14. aud yet believe that there is a *Purgatory* after this life , where men muft be be *tormented* and suffer *extream pains* there, to expiate such *venial fins*, as their prayers and *pennances* here could not doe; yea is here made to wonder how any that believes such a thing, can ever have *true peace*, or *comfort in the-world*, but doe either take it as a *fiction*, or forget themselves when they are *chearfull*; where the fear of such a *place*, the uncertainty of *releafe*, and how long a *term* it may be er this *purging worke be compleat*, (when their own *writers* assigne no lesse time, then 10000 *Years* as needfull to *satisfy* for some *fins*,) and leaft it prove a *reall hell*, muft ftill be a prefent terrour; nor can he believe that such poffibly doe *credit* themfelves herein, who affume this power to *change the condition of the dead*, fince were it really *believed*, that the *keyes* of fuch a *prifon* were here in mens hand, and could, by the largeft *dotations to the Romish Church*, get a fafe outgate thence, it were not ftrang, to fee the *temporall ftate of Crifendome* in a fhort time made over to thefe, and fhould Judge they were in a ftrang manner indead priviledged by the whole refidue of men, who by fuch a *power over the world to come* can make fo eafy a *purchafe over this alfo which is prefent*. 9. He finds & is fure he could never get his *reafon* and *confcience* brought to fuch a *faith*, even tho he made a *fimulate* profeffion herein, of that *pretended fupremacy of Peter as Bishop of Rome*, on which the whole *frame* and ftructure of the *pa-*

pacy.

pacy leans , and the *vertue of all the pardons and absolutions* founded theron , on which so many have adventured into an other world except he would thus *build on the sand* only , but not on *the rock.* 10. He finds also how such an *erection* of the *Gospell Church* in her militant state here , *as* the *Papacy* in its *complexe frame* is , unite in such an *head* , as the *Pope* , who as the *sole vicegerent of Christ* in the earth , is at once invested with a *civill Monarchy* , and *universall impire* over the Church, to *impose* , and *judge* in the highest transactions that relate to the *eternall state;* and *immortall souls* of men , is a thing that as to *matter of right* is as *forreign to the Scripture* and incompatible therwith , as *Mahumitanisme* can be , and as to *matter of fact* is a *trust* that no *created being* could ever exerce. 11. he sees & is sure that he must either lose sight both of the *rule* , and *spirit of the Gospell* , or have a just abhorrence at that way , where he should be inevitably *involved in a virtual consent* , *and accession* to all that *cruelty* and *blood* which for so many ages hath been shed therin , when its so clear that this was no *exorbitance* only of *practice* , but a native result of their *tenets*, and *principles*, and not only *dispensed* with , but counted an highly *meritorious* service ; yea when it is sure that under no *secular government* of the most *tyrannicall state* that ever was in the world , hath such *arbitrary violence*, and *oppression* been exerced , or so much innocent

nocent *blood* fhed , as by this party. 12. And tho his judgment ftood indetermined and in an *equall ballance* upon this great controverfie , he could not exerce reafon, and not fee upon what *hand* fuch a *decifion* is as was in *Solomons time* of the *true mother of the child* , and who does moft *ruthfully* feek to intereffe themfelves in the im-minent *hazard* of the *Chriftian faith*, and under leaft influence of any *temporall motives* does this day ftand for the *truth* and *fubftance of Chiftia-nity* , and plead that it be not deftroyed in envy and hatred to them ; or on what fide it is like-ways that this manner of *conqueft* is moft follow-ed to gain men to the profeffion of the truth by a *prevailing evidence* of their own *light* and jud-gment herein , and to require their exacteft *per-fonall tryall* , and *inquiry* about the fame.

In the 3d place, tho he fees there can be no pretence of *doctrinall wavering* about the *Re-formed* religion , and finds it not eafy to com-prehend how in one and the fame *age* , wher-in the *truth* hath fo brightly fhined , this way of *Popery* , fhould have *prevalence,* or gain ground any more by *feduction* from *arguments to the rea-fon* or *confcience of* any ; yet fince it is an *hower of temptation* , and of *fainting* , above all that hath been hitherto known , and mens eyes ar-reafted with fuch a *profpect* of the time , as is like to *ftagger* the *faith* of the moft eftablifhed, he is thus preffed , as one of the higheft *duties*

C 4   *of*

of this day , to know and search out what may afford greatest *assistance* to his *faith* , from the *dispensations of providence* therin, and to know the *evidence* and *strenth* of such *reflections* as these are for this *end.*

.   1. That its sure , as the *smallest things* which the Lord does afford , to strenthen and support against such a *storme* , should be seriously *improven* , and taken to heart ; so does it lay us in the way of that *promise* for having *greater things* given to our *observation* ; yea that now is the time when such as have been most comforted by the word of *promise* , may be put to the forest *tryal* in their *faith* of any , to keep off stumbling at the *worke of providence* , and be thus tryed according to the measure of these *confirmations.*

.   2. Tho the *Churches declinings* under greatest measures of *light* may be too visible , and that religion gains not by *persecution* as formerly , with such an amazing chang as is now in her external condition, yet sees it to be no strang thing, when most signal *warnings* have gone before of such a tryal with too evident *dispositions* towards the same and discovery of its approach in all the *causes* therof ; yea might be forseen by all , that the *holy God* would not still bear with an *impure* , and *uninlivned profession* of the *pure* and *glorious truth of Christianity* , which hath now long been one of the most sad , and mortall *signs* in the *publick state* of religion; nor can it be found
that

that ever any *Church* did decline and fall from the *purity* of the truth and lose ground herein by externall *perfecution*, where a judicial departure of its *life* and *power* did not remarkably goe before; so as it is not of late this hath been too clearly *prefaged*, that som dark and unusual measure of tryall from *Antichrift*, and that *ultima clades* of the *Reformed Churches*, was drawing near, which would be fore er it had done its worke.

3. He sees also, how this present *hower* is not more searching and *dark*, then it may be *clear* herewith, 1. that now after the *issue* of that oppofition, which was betwixt the Christian faith in the *firft entry* of the Gospell and that dying Apoftate *Church of the Jewes*, and *next* with the *Pagan Impire*, after that new erection of the Gospell Church among the *Gentils*, which is now over; so is the greateft *tryall* of the *latter* dayes fixed on the *decifion* of that long depending *controverfie betwixt Chrift and Antichrift.* 2. That according to the Scripture we muft believe that as *after the manner of Egypt*, that glorious *triumph* and *delivery* of the *Church from Antichrift* will be furlie carryed on, so the more near it comes to the *laft affault*, and when this falls in to have its *proper roome* in the *frame* and adminiftration of providence, the greater *extremitie, terrour* and *darkneffe* may be expected also, as hath not been in any fuch manner formerly, yea with that *unite* and *formidable conjunction* of ftrenth and *growing fucceffe* of

C 5

this adverfary for a time, as the moft eftablifhed Chriftians may be in hazard to ftagger. 3. That now is the day wherin the Lord will have men know what it is to have the *Bible* as the alone *fecurity* of the *Proteftant religion*, on which they muft intirely reft no leffe then it is the *fole rule* and *ftandard* therof, which is a *tryall* worthy of all that expenfe of the *pain*, *anguish*, and *wreftlings*, that can now poffibly attend the fame.

4. Whilft the *great ftandard of Antichrifts Kingdome* is vifibly fet up and brought to the *open field*, as its this day in the **Church of France**, and all human help taken out of fight; yet does he fee herewith, 1 how this now is concluded, as the moft *infallible remedy* to recover *Popery*, and that *argument*, to which they truft more then to *Peters keyes* to wit thefe *fanguinary lawes* by the *fword*, and *rack*, which they have again betaken themfelves to, tho fuch an *argument* the Scripture never knew, which fober *heathens* would abhorr, and gives up the *credite* of all religion to *Atheifm*. 2. That there can be no more evidence of a *defperate and finking caufe* then is here, and how nothing elfe can fupport it but thefe *weapons* which are not againft the *Confcience*, or by any terrours of the *2d death*, but of the *firft*. 3. that this is fuch an *argument*, (if they have not in a ftrang manner forgot,) which hath within thefe 100 *Years* been fo fully *anfwered*, and by fuch an immediate appearence of God in the *Kingdome*

dome of *France*, that according to thefe meafures of cruelty againft the *Proteftants* there , fo was it returned in a *deludge of their own blood* , yea thus both the publick ftate of the Church and faith of the faints in the truth more deeply rooted ; and tho we yet fee not the end of *thefe wonders* and the *darke fide* only of the difpenfations of fuch a day , yet doe we know this *fore rod* on the Church is but as the *faw* and *axe in the carpenters hand*, who fhall never *undoe* that *glorious worke* which Chrift hath done and is ftill further perfecting on the ruins of *Antichrifts Kingdome.*

5. Tho fome unufuall *deeps* and *methods of fubtilty* be now on foot alfo againft the truth , yet he cannot but fee how nothing could more effectually tend to confirm the *proteftant caufe* and take the *credite of popery* off the confcience of thefe in their *own profeffion* who are confiderate and in the leaft ferious herein ; when the world muft thus fee , 1 how eafy its for fuch to take any *meafure and latitude* in the *doctrinals* of their profeffion , when this can moft ferve the juncture of fuch a time and *highten* or *narrow* the controverfy betwixt them and the *Reformed* Church at their pleafure , fo as to *facrifice* the *Church of Rome* unto the *Court of Rome* , if no leffe can fecure that end. 2. That the moft horrid *Turkifh Slavery* over mens bodies comes no fuch lenth , as that ftrang *claime* that thefe.

now

now make of an *abſolute impire* over mens conſcience by the *ſword*, and to put them to ſuch a
tribute of their obedience , and they ſhall then
be ſecure, if they but come the lenth-to ſin a-
gainſt their light , and adventure on ſo ſmall a
thing as to goe to *Hell and periſh eternally*, ſince
its an externall and ſimulate profeſſion of ſuch
a way they doe thus inforce from theſe , whom
they ſee cannot in faith be perſwaded hereof.
3. Yea it hath been too viſible how much
that *maſter-plot*, and *ingine*, hath in theſe times
been working, to take men firſt off all *ſenſe* of
religion , and deſtroy them in the *morals of Chriſtianity*, to make this *conqueſt* more eaſy , that
ſuch may have no *inward defence* and ſupport a-
gainſt the terrour of *human violence* , yea in this
way , when they have ſought how to *divide Pro-
teſtants among themſelves* and betwixt *Rulers* and
them , this ſeams the *laſt* and greateſt ingine of
all , how to *divide betwixt them and their God*, and
act the ſame plot, which was laid betwixt *Balack*
and *Balaam*, as knowing that its no naked ſhew
or profeſſion of the *Reformed religion* they nead
fear,ſo much as that *old proteſtant ſpirit* in the *power
& life* therof, before which their intereſt could never ſtand , and dreads nothing ſo much as the
reviving hereof, which as the *hand-writing upon the
wall* did ever more threaten the fatall ruine of
that Kingdome , then any *human power* or
ſtrenth.

6. Here

6. Here also he finds just cause of astonishment, how *Kings or great men* in the earth should give their *power* to support the *Romish interest*, that hath been so visibly destructive to theirs, when its not possible to deny how its *first* advance and progresse to that *supreme hight*, which it once attained, and the *declining* of the *civill impire*, did by the same *steps* goe together, untill *Magistracy* was turned as unto a *dead image and shaddow*, except its being *enlivened* by their *breath* and authority, as it was during the whole *hight* of that Antichristian power ; nor will it be denyed that in these *late times* the *French Monarchy* was never more near its dissolution in its *right line*, then by the *Catholick league* there; and would seem not easy to be forgot, how *Henry the 3d*, who had most sought to crush the *Protestants* there in pursuance of that *league*, was at last constrained to flee to such for help, or by whom he was *killed*; and that *Heroick Prince Henry the 4.* was first *stabbed in the mouth* and then in the *heart* ; yea that the publick *records* of that *nation* cannot possibly deny how the *house of Burbon* owes its *power* and *preservation* more to the *Protestants*, (without whom it had been fully extinct,) then *Ahasuerus* did to *Mordecai* the *Jew* for what he found written in the *Chronicles of Persia*, when the *decree* was then past to destroy all the seed of the *Jewes*.

7. As

7. As in no times paſt was ever a greater *expectation* then is now , which way the *ſcale* will, turn , and what will be the end of theſe *wonders* , when the *neareſt events* of Providence are ſo darke and amazing; ſo does he find this, in ſome eztraordinare way called for , *to be ſtill, and ſee what God will doe for his Church* , and with humble confidence look for ſome *diſpenſation* as hath not, hitherto been in this extreme exigence , and tho: he doe not appeare in that *way* and *manner* as in *former times* , that it ſhall be in a way more, ſignally *glorʼous* , beyond what hath formerly been ; yea does in *faith* thus judge , that then is the *Churches day broke* , and hath found the ſure way of *her ſtrenth* , and *right lith of duty* , when her *hope* and *confidence* is taken of all *viſible refuges* and intirely ſetled on her *inviſible head*, and his *promiſe* put to *ſuite* by *prayer without fainting* herein. It is ſure the *truth & faithſullneſſe* of God ſtands ingadged for *Antichriſts fall* , as well as for *ſalvation by Chriſt* ; and ſince he hath ſaid this *adverſary* ſhall be *broke* and brought down , it muſt ſurely be , *tho the duſt of the ground* ſhould riſe for this end, and now is the *faith* of the ſaints called for becoming the greatneſſe of ſuch an *aſſurance* , on which are the *eyes of men* , of their own *conſcience* , of the *elect Angels* , yea of the *glorious God* , to ſee who does indeed *credit* him in this day, when there is no ſenſible ſupport herein; and

tho

(47.)

tho it is now like to ſhake ſore the *departure* of
many from the *faith* who had ſome viſible profeſſion therof, yet may it be hoped for, that the
turn of the next tyde ſhall bring in *moe*, with a
ſolid and *true increaſe to the Church*, then theſe
ſad dayes doe now *take off.*

CHARACT. VI. It is thus a *confirmed
Chriſtian* ſhould be ſpecially conſidered, as one
who is not only at *reſt on the known certainty of his faith*, but is *ready to render ſome account*
of the *ſolid rationall grounds* and *demonſtrations* hereof, *unto all who ask* after the ſame, and doth
thus judge, 1 that theſe are the *proper* and *appointed means* which the Lord hath afforded for the
greateſt *confirmation* of mens faith within time,
yea preferable to any *externall miracles*, which
are more extraordinare and remott *aſſiſtances* therto. 2. That theſe are given as ſo great an
helper to his joy, and *excitment* of his affections
to *follow the Lord fully*, as makes him wonder
how the greatneſſe of theſe things, which men
are called to believe, can come near their thoughts,
and yet not more taken up about this *confirming worke.* 3. That the too viſible neglect herof; both with reſpect to the *youth* and *commu-
nity of profeſſours* in the Church, ſeems one of
the ſad, and *fundamentall defects* of this day.
The *reaſons* hereof, with ſome clear view of
theſe *means* which might moſt anſwer ſuch an
end, are *briefly offered*, in this *preceding worke.*
CHA-

CHARACT. VII. A truely *confirmed Christian* may in the *last place* be herein alſo conſi-dered, as ſuch whoſe *faith being oft tryed* through all theſe *ſtages of Chriſtianity* he hath been taken; hath ſome *proper record* of the moſt *choiſe*, and *ſignall confirmations of his life*, to improve the ſame not only for his *own ſupport* in that *laſt warfare of death*, but for *ſtrenthning the faith of others*; wherin he does thus judge, 1 that there could be no true ſupport or relief from *religion* here in the earth, if it cannot bear out then, and that *death* is the great *touchſtone* and *tryall*, when the true *value* and difference betwixt things of an *eternall truth* and *ſubſtance*, and the things of this *world*, will be beſt ſeen. 2. He reckons each real Chriſtian, by his profeſſion then *ſiſted* and accountable, even by ſome *explicit perſonall teſtimony*, to put to his *ſeal that God is true*, and bear the ſame witneſſe with his *laſt* and *dying breath* to the *truth of Chriſtianity*, which he gave in the whole courſe of his life; and of that *joy*, *complacence* and *aſſurance of mind*, which he hath found, and now hath in the way of truth, ſo as to preſſe the ſame on his *deareſt relations* as their alone true intereſt. 3. He ſees alſo, how *honorable* it is for the Lord, that ſuch whoſe faith hath been oft *tryed*, (and when thus with *joy* and *admiration* he can look back on the moſt preſſing and conſpicuous *conflicts* of time,) ſhould have it their laſt worke to pay

in

in some *tribute of praise*, unto *him* whose *word* &
promise unto them did yet *never fail*. 4. He accounts the more *weighty tryalls* he hath been carryed thorow in his Christian warfare, doth both
give more accesse to this *service*, and adds more
to the *value* of such a *testimony*. 5. He judgeth
this one special way and advantage, wherby *one*
generation might declare the truth and faithfullnesse of
God unto an other, in a family line and relation, to shew
forth thus that the *Lord is upright*, that *he is their*
rock, and *with him is no unrighteousnesse*; yea which
should be matter of unspeakable joy, when now
in his *turn* he can say that such hath the Lord
been to him, what was *Davids* dying words 1
Kings. 1:14. Who hath delivered my soul out of all di-
stresse, how that in no trouble or *exigence* of his
life he was ever left without a *door of outgate*;
and thus also with *Caleb Josh. 14:10.* to give
in some such *wittnesse for God* I am now near
the *close of time*, and does *testify*, that the *word*
of his truth, and promise he hath surely *accompli-*
shed, which hath brought *me safe* and *honourably*
through, when such as did *dicredit* the same by
misbelief, and sought after another *refuge*, found
all *their confidences fail.* 6. And knowing like-
ways how great a *suprizall death* may be, and
that such as have *shined* in their day, may yet set
under a *cloud* and goe silent off the *stage*, he judgeth it the more needfull to have such a *piece of*
his dying worke prepared, as one of the choif-

est

eft *legacies* he can bequath to his furviving friends,
in a *feafon* when it hath ufually the greateft advantage of *weight* and acceptance: it being ftill
qualified with *Chriftian prudence*, and *humble fo-
briety*, fo as all may fee its whole intent is to
commend to mens confcience the *way of truth* and
godlineffe and not themfelves, and thus only
direct, for the *proper ufe*, and improvment of
their neareft relations. I know it may be ftrang
to fome, what is fpoke upon this head; but as
its fure the prefent day hath its *duty*, and each
time of our life hath fome *proper worke*, fo I
humbly judge, that this feems to fall in as the
laft fervice of a dying Chriftian to his generation,
to *deliver of his hand the truth* which he had received and hath oft *proven*, with his *confirmatory feal* and *teftimony* therto, and now in fome
more then ordinare way called for in this hower
of great darkneffe, when if that fecurity of the
abfolute promifes ftood not good to the Church,
we might fear *religion* might quickly wear out,
and *truth* perifh from the earth; and as fo folemn and weighty a thing fhould be mannaged
with much humble prudence, fo it may be judged that no ferious and *obferving* Chriftian but
hath fome peculiare *ingadgments* under which they
find themfelves fifted even beyond others, yea
fome fuch *fingulare confirmations* in the *journall*
of their life, that fhould be not eafy to *hide* under
the ground, where the *ftrenthning of others* here-
by

by is conceirned , and that such should not then leave the *croffe of Jefus Chrift* at a *loffe* , or part therwith without their *teftimony* , which hath left them at fo great an *advantage*. And though this is not to offer particulare *rules* in fuch a duty, but that *Chriftian wisdome* muft direct herein , as the prefent *cafe is circumftantiate* , yet might it be hoped , were this more taken to heart , it should be a singulare *mean* , to put a more deep impreffion of mens *dying worke* on their own spirit , even whilft they are in *health,* to *excite* their furviving friends , and to keep *religion* thus *alive* in a *family ftate* , and *relation* , and gain a more venerable *refpect* to the fame on mens confcience , yea to *fix* alfo ftronger *ingadgments* on the *fucceeding offfpring*.

Thus is prefented here a short Idea of the *folid and judicious worke of Chriftian confirmation in the truth,* under thefe forgoing *Characters,* to shew how rare an atteanment of religion this is , yea to prefent herein a speciall *feries* and *fcale* of the greateft *fteps in this confirmatory worke* , by which it should be followed , and where none of thefe may be parted from other , though fome be of an higher and more abfolute ufe for fuch an end. And if it should be objected here, what needs any fuch expenfe of *time* or *pains* in this cafe , when its fure the effentiall truths of the Gofpell are not *queftioned* , and that without *internall evidence* of the spirit , no externall means of this kind can

be

be of ufe. I know that its the alone worke of the *holy Ghoſt* , to beget a *divine* and *ſupernaturall faith*; without which the furtheſt *light* , and *objective evidence* , though backed with a continued diſpenſation of *externall miracles*, could never bear Chriſtians out, either as to *duty* or *comfort* , in their paſſage thorow time; yea nothing is in the leaſt here to ſubject the *credite* of our *faith* to mens *rationall comprehenſion* , but rather tends to enervate wholly the ſtrenth of any ſuch *tenet* and take off all pretence for the ſame : But its ſure alſo, I muſt quite all *ſolid ſecurity* in the way of religion , and any clear founding in the *light and certainty of the Scripture* , or admitt theſe things as undenyable, 1 that *ſupernaturall faith* is the moſt *highly rationall light* thats within time , and that none who profeſſe the name of Chriſt can be of ſo low a *ſize,* as ſhould not be preſſed and *excited* to be much about this *ground worke* of knowing the *truth* , and *principles* of their profeſſion upon its *own evidence* ; yea are thus called *as new born babes to drink in the ſincere milk of the word* , 1 **Pet. 2.** Which, as its clearly in the *originall*, is the *rationall milk of the word*, to be thus received no leſſe on *conviction* and *certainty* of the judgment, then with the out going of their *affections.* 2. That as its not conceivable how a *true* and *firme aſſent* can be to *divine truth*, but on its *known certainty,* ſo here is no *reſolving* of the Chriſtians faith on the ſtrongeſt *rationall evidences* hereof, of , yet muſt it ſtill be *reſolved* on the *teſtimony of God*, made clear & *evident to them* to be ſuch. 3. It is ſure alſo , the Lord hath not given ſo large a meaſure of theſe *grounds* and *demonſtrations* of his truth with ſuch *redoubled arguments* of that kind , to be of ſo ſmall regard , as is with moſt , but for ſome *great* , and *univerſall uſe* hereof to the wholl Church, and knew how needfull ſuch *aſſi-ſtances* to the faith of his people would be, whilſt they are on the earth. 4. That theſe *means* , which tend moſt convincingly to found a *ratio-nall aſſurence* in the judgment , are the proper *vehicle of the Spirit of God* , by which his *ſealing worke* , ſhould be both ſought and expected ; nor can I judge how the credite and uſe hereof ſhould be ſo ſmall , and not on the ſame ground quite any *externall ordinance* of the Goſpell , which without the Spirit of the Lord can never profite , nor how we ſhould expect and ſuite his *confirming worke* on the ſoul , when theſe greateſt confirming means, which he hath given to the Church , have no juſt weight ; but o how wonderfull a teacher is the holy Ghoſt , when ſuch ordinare means fail , and are *inac-ceſſable* , by furniſhing his people then with theſe ſtrongeſt *arguments of love and power* , who hav-ing had but ſmall *meaſures of light* , yet were not unfaithfull to improve the ſmalleſt degree of ſuch a talent. 5. Yea ſo great a thing is it , to at-tain a ſolid *faith of things* wholly *remott from our*

ſenſe;

] fo far *above* the reach and *a*
r to have an abfolute relyan
re , for our prefent and et
non affent can anfwer, wl
iet of the foul muſt needs ly
perfuafion hereof. 6. It is to
the *praΕticall uſe of ſuch a m*
d *in the Church* , that all wh
; might no leffe know the
f *the foundation of their faitl.*
then the *generall articles* o
the moſt ufuall inſtruΕting
olly about the *noetick part*
s not that ſerious regard t
part hereof on mens conſcien
reſtriΕted to a few who are r
d; and of an inquiſitive ſpir
rtainty of the truth, and for
abundant helps of this kind
, ſeem more peculiarly d
the Chriſtian faith in the
y then ſpread and prevail, b
ereof to the judgment, ma
t *of God*, more then by *extr*
r knew they otherwiſe what
put by imbracing the truth w
lerſtanding, no leffe then o
But if it be objeΕted, it is n
where religion is *planted in*
controllable *publick profeſſi*

support of *humane lawes* ; I know no weight this can
have, except that should be admitt therwith, *quod nunc
nafcuntur Chriftiani, fed non fiunt.* 7. Yea is it not fure,
(tho it feems little underftood ,) that the *primary
grounds* and *evidences* of our faith are not only as to their
end demonftrative of the truth and divinity of the Scripture , but are upon the *matter* fuch *demonftrations* alfo
which moft natively refult from the fame by- infallible *confequence,* aud are thus to be accounted not as *human* .ut *divine arguments,* given us by the fpirit of God.
8. I shall but further add , how fuch as doe ferioufly
ponder things, will find this *demonftration* to be not more
important then clear , that to be a *confirmed Chriftian*
and a *confirmed Proteftant* are *convertible terms* ; and that
if thefe as are under that deplorable bondage and *darkneffe of popery* were but once *awaked* to fee the *truth* &
certainty of the Chriftian faith , by its *intrinfick* and
objective evidence , and taken off that brutish credulity and dependance on the alone credite of others herein , it might be faid the *ftrongeft ingine* to hold up that
profeffion were then broke, and should fee the *doctrine*
and *rule of faith* to be of fuch *full* and *perfpicuous evidence*
from the Scripture, as without *blafphemy* they could
not feek from the Lord to give them a *plainer rule,* then
what he hath there given.

READER.

ITs like *yow may think ftrang, how thefe few sheets in
the clofe fall in here , after the forgoing part was fini-
shed ; but tho they meet in one defigne and intereft, yet
was not this then intended untill the former was done , and
if it might tend to a folid ufe and fruit unto any , I shall
forbear a further Apology herein. I may trulie fay , the
weight of the fubject hath carryed it fome further lenth
then was defigned , when I fo much fought to be short , as*

any thing of this kind, that through my defire
my unneceffare multiplying of words, I fear
make fome things feem a litle dark at the firft
I hope not upon any ferious perufall of the fame.
I muft further crave leave to add; 1 that when
& view of the great affiftances and confirma-
aith is here offered, which thefe of the low-
of the Church, might with that advantage
in a few howers, by reading it fome times
be fo far impreffed on their mind and judg-
they could give fome clear and judicious ac-
it may be by fuch but ferioufly weighed & taken
hat conceirn the ufe hereof is; 2. That I would
e alfo it were a moft fpeciall fervice for the truth
, to have fome fhort Directory and remem-
he great acts of the Lord and monuments
idence now under the New Teftament, in that
orth as might moft tend to fome univerfall ufe
the Church. I confeffe my defire preffed me to fome
rein, with intent to have joyned it to this worke,
with much conviction laid this wholly afide,
ther appearence that way, fo is it with an
re, that fome more qualifyed, might take
under their hand fo great a fervice both for
tion and pofterity. It is fure the Lord hath
people to be tought the greatneffe of his workes
he precepts of his word; and as no duty is more
this under the Old Teftament both as to Publick
inftruction, fo are we no leffe accountable in
nes for this improvment of fuch as are of known,
d uncontrollable evidence, and fhould be the
age to have that folemne remembrance kept up
not a few, but the very multitude within the
it be as a publick Library and Repofitory of the

FINIS.

www.ingramcontent.com/pod-product-compliance
Lightning Source LLC
Chambersburg PA
CBHW020009030726
47500CB00002B/508